CONCISE
LINCOLN
LIBRARY

—

EDITED BY RICHARD W. ETULAIN,
SARA VAUGHN GABBARD, AND
SYLVIA FRANK RODRIGUE

MICHAEL S. GREEN

Lincoln and the Election of 1860

Southern Illinois University Press
Carbondale and Edwardsville

14 13 12 11   4 3 2 1

The Concise Lincoln Library has been made possible
in part through a generous donation by the Leland E.
and LaRita R. Boren Trust.

Library of Congress Cataloging-in-Publication Data
Green, Michael S.
Lincoln and the election of 1860 / Michael S. Green.
      p. cm. — (Concise Lincoln library)
Includes bibliographical references and index.
ISBN-13: 978-0-8093-3035-5 (cloth : alk. paper)
ISBN-10: 0-8093-3035-0 (cloth : alk. paper)
ISBN-13: 978-0-8093-8636-9 (ebook)
ISBN-10: 0-8093-8636-4 (ebook)
1. Lincoln, Abraham, 1809–1865—Political career before
1861. 2. Presidents—United States—Election—1860.
3. Political campaigns—United States—History—
19th century. 4. United States—Politics and govern-
ment—1857–1861. 5. Republican Party (U.S. : 1854–)—
History—19th century. 6. Presidential candidates—
United States—Biography. 7. Presidents—United
States—Biography. I. Title.
E457.G83 2011
973.7092—dc22   2010054455

Printed on recycled paper. ♻
The paper used in this publication meets the minimum
requirements of American National Standard for Information Sciences—Permanence of Paper for Printed
Library Materials, ANSI Z39.48-1992. ∞

To Deborah

CONTENTS

PREFACE

When historian David Herbert Donald wrote about generations trying to "get right with Lincoln," he described almost
any subject related to Abraham Lincoln. How Lincoln became the
Republican nominee in 1860 provides an example in a life writ large.
Donald's biography depicts Lincoln as generally passive and funda-
mentally Whiggish, even as a Republican. William C. Harris's study
of Lincoln's pre-presidential career points to his combination of conservatism and progressivism. Other historians cite his ambition, that
"little engine" that motivated him, and his political savvy. Almost
every historian notes his capacity for growth. Where historians locate
him on the Republican spectrum ranges from J. G. Randall's view
of him as conservative to Stephen Oates's depiction of him as radical
at heart, with others falling in between.

Even if they sometimes strike historians otherwise, these ideas
about Lincoln are not mutually exclusive. What follows is an attempt to combine information and diverse points of view into a short,
readable narrative and analysis of how Lincoln won the election of
1860. I do not deny Lincoln's faults: he managed to use other people,
although in a friendly way designed to do no personal harm; less
admirably, he made statements that are racist by any definition, although less racist than those voiced by others in his time. They also
show that he was incredibly human and often distant, making him all
the easier to analyze and all the harder to understand. In seeking the
presidency—and let there be no doubt, Lincoln sought it—he demonstrated great political and managerial acumen. He remained true

to Republican principles. He acted in part out of his own ambitions but also to squelch those of Stephen Douglas, his longtime rival in Illinois politics, who troubled him as both the potential Democratic nominee and a possible compromise candidate to whom Republicans might turn—if, in Lincoln's opinion, they placed instant political gratification over the party's and the country's long-term good.

Thus, this study emphasizes Lincoln's role in this election—what he did and did not do. It takes into account what went on among his Republican friends and opponents as well as in the Democratic and Constitutional Union Parties. Above all, it demonstrates Lincoln's commitment to his party's principles and, most significant for the election of 1860, his unparalleled political ability.

Lincoln probably said, "That reminds me of a story," less often than he is credited with saying it. But, in Lincoln's spirit, let me start that way to explain this book and offer some thanks. A few years ago, an effort led by Pat and Merlin Sumner, among others, to form a Civil War roundtable where I live—in Las Vegas, which may shock those who cannot imagine scholarly interests there—led to a call from the group's first speaker, John Y. Simon, the editor of Ulysses S. Grant's papers. He became a mentor and friend and recommended me to Sylvia Frank Rodrigue of Southern Illinois University Press for a variety of projects. I wish Professor Simon were still here; his well-known mix of wisdom, sarcasm, and humor would have made this a better book.

A few years after that fortuitous phone call, my mother-in-law, Lenora Young, moved to Portland, Oregon, to be closer to her son and his family. She went to a lecture on Lincoln and the West near her home and introduced herself to the speaker, who gave her his card to give to me. This led to a friendship with one of the West's most distinguished scholars, Richard Etulain, who invited me to be part of this series. He has been a model editor, as many historians have learned, and I look forward to sharing many years of Lincolniana and western Americana with him—or, to rephrase that, learning from him.

Dick, Sylvia, and Sara Vaughn Gabbard started this series and invited me to be part of it. They provided detailed readings of this manuscript and displayed tact, friendship, and a wonderful knowledge of history—all of which I deeply appreciate. As executive editor for the press, Sylvia also has done much to shepherd this book to publication, and I wish to thank her and her great staff.

I also owe a great debt to librarians, especially those at the University of Nevada, Las Vegas, and the College of Southern Nevada. A month at The Huntington Library, researching a different project, gave me a few spare minutes to work on this book, and I am grateful to Peter Blodgett and the marvelous staff in the Ahmanson Reading Room and in Reader Services. Thanks go to Robert C. Ritchie, Carolyn Powell, and Susi Krasnoo for their help with the Los Angeles Corral of Westerners Fellowship. Scott Daniels and the staff at the Oregon Historical Society made time spent there rewarding and productive.

I am blessed with good friends who also toil in nineteenth-century history. I am indebted, for their advice and example, to Heather Cox Richardson, Andrew Slap, John David Smith, Scott Stabler, Michael Vorenberg, and Xi Wang. Ralph Roske immersed me in this era, and Eric Foner made sure I knew it better than I thought I could.

Greg Borchard again proved his friendship and tolerance by reading this book and making suggestions—and providing material from the book he is contributing to this series on the relationship between Lincoln and Horace Greeley. Yanek Mieczkowski and I became close friends as beginning graduate students at Columbia University and remain so even after he carefully read this book. Where I have heeded my colleagues and peers, this manuscript benefited; where I ignored them, it will suffer.

My understanding, such as it is, of politics owes a great deal to my friendships with Mary Lou Foley and Michael Epling, Sara and Ralph Denton, and their families. That they have so many of Lincoln's virtues and few if any of his vices is evident to all who know them.

I can say the same of my father, Robert Green, and my late mother, Marsha, both of whom inspired me with their love and pride as well as with their belief that having a lot of books around the house was a good thing.

Since she is the subject of the dedication, she is first, but here I have saved the best for last. I want to thank Deborah Young, for everything.

LINCOLN AND THE ELECTION OF 1860

PRELUDE TO A TURNING POINT

"God help me, God help me," Abraham Lincoln said late the night of November 6, 1860. From the election returns arriving in Springfield, Illinois, Lincoln learned what he and other Republicans had anticipated for the past month: he would be the next president. Little did he imagine how much help he actually would need. After going home and telling his wife, "Mary, Mary, we are elected," he mapped out a cabinet that drew on his party's regions, leanings, and political antecedents. Six weeks later, South Carolina seceded; six other southern states followed suit before Lincoln took office on March 4, 1861.[1]

Thanks to his abilities and the swirl of events around him, Lincoln became the president who guided the United States through the Civil War. One of the least experienced men to occupy the White House—briefly a militia captain, a four-term state legislator, a one-term congressman, a veteran attorney, and a Whig and Republican operative—he evolved into the Great Emancipator, a commander-in-chief whose strategy won the war for the North, and an architect of an expansion of industry and government power that reshaped American life. Throughout the secession winter, though, he expected not that series of events but that a tide of southern unionism would engulf secessionists. The firing on Fort Sumter and the ensuing war that killed 620,000 proved him wrong. While hindsight always suggests clearer answers, it shows that the threads holding the Union together were thin, and the 1860 election snapped them. The divide over slavery had grown too large for increasingly sectional parties and leaders to bridge, and understanding what happened in 1860 requires an understanding of what produced the times and the men who made them.

The First Party System

The Founding Fathers bridged the gap over slavery, but not easily. The Second Continental Congress approved the Declaration of Independence only after cutting Thomas Jefferson's criticism of slavery from his draft but also temporarily ended the African slave trade. As the American Revolution turned colonies into states, the writers of state constitutions in the North abolished slavery gradually and with little controversy, due to its limited impact on their region's economy and society. Under the Articles of Confederation, the Northwest Ordinance of 1787 banned slavery from the territories that later became Ohio, Indiana, Illinois, Michigan, and Wisconsin. According to James Madison, at the Constitutional Convention, "the institution of slavery and its implication formed the line of discrimination." The Constitution required states to return fugitive slaves to their owners, kept Congress from barring the African slave trade for twenty years after ratification, and counted each slave as three-fifths of a person for determining each state's members of the House of Representatives and electoral college—all advantages to the South. In turn, the document never mentioned slavery, suggesting the Framers' desire to avoid the topic and possibly their dislike for it. Delegate James Wilson expected a future ban on the slave trade to lead to abolition: "Yet the lapse of a few years, and Congress will have power to exterminate slavery from within our borders."[2]

Whether or not Wilson divined the future, the other Founders' intentions became central to the political developments leading up to the 1860 election and the events that followed. Clearly, though, the Constitution's authors never envisioned the interlocking factors that prompted the disputes over slavery that characterized American politics for a significant part of the nineteenth century. First, in 1793, the cotton gin's invention reduced the labor required for separating seeds from the cotton, speeding production. Other improvements fostered industrialization, making it easier to convert raw materials into finished products and to reach markets to sell them. With the demand for more cotton came the need for more land on which to grow it, prompting southerners to push west with their slaves into Kentucky, Tennessee, Alabama, and Mississippi, expanding the institution beyond the Framers' expectations. In 1793, wanting to protect their economy and investments, and with the possibility of Congress banning the African slave trade as soon as the Constitution allowed, southerners won passage of a fugitive slave law, requiring northerners to help return runaways to their owners.

Blossoming over issues unrelated to slavery, political parties represented another break with the Framers' expectations—and, eventually, became inseparable from slavery. In the early and mid-1790s, the first party system developed over ideological differences between the first secretary of state, Jefferson, and the first secretary of the treasury, Alexander Hamilton. Jefferson's Republicans advocated a limited government with most of its power in congressional hands and an agricultural economy; Hamilton's Federalists preferred more federal involvement in building an economy based on industry and bondholders. These disagreements went beyond ideology: each party expected to destroy the other, given that neither group recognized the other as legitimate. Jefferson and Hamilton saw each other not merely as political opponents competing for votes and power but as traitors to the new Republic's well-being. Thus, Jefferson declared in his inauguration, "We are all republicans; we are all federalists," but sounded a far different note when he later wrote privately, "I shall . . . sink federalism into an abyss from which there shall be no resurrection for it."[3]

With the Federalist Party's demise after the 1816 election, the first party system collapsed, but the issue of slavery gained new resonance. Missouri's quest for admission as a slave state in 1819 prompted a sectional debate, resolved with a compromise that admitted Missouri and Maine, maintaining a balance between free and slave states, with slavery otherwise banned north of Missouri's southern border. Jefferson wrote that "this momentous question, like a fire bell in the night, awakened and filled me with terror." More significant, a Georgia congressman complained to a northern colleague who fought efforts to allow slavery in Missouri, "You have kindled a fire which all the waters of the ocean cannot put out, which seas of blood can only extinguish." Less than two generations later, northerners and southerners proved him right.[4]

The Second Party System

Slavery had little to do with the rise of new political parties, except that many participants in those parties hoped to limit the issue's scope or ignore it entirely. However, old divisions died hard, and connections to slavery, even when relegated to the political sidelines, proved inescapable. Federalists disappeared as a party, but believers in expansive government and industrial growth found little refuge among those committed to Jefferson's belief in limited government and a mostly agricultural economy. Also, southerners and some northerners shared the conviction that Jeffersonian Republicans eliminated the Federalists by adopting too many of their views and expanding federal power beyond wise or constitutional limits. In turn, their beliefs hardened and narrowed beyond Jefferson's intentions.[5]

Mainly from this strain of Jefferson's ideas, the Democratic Party emerged. The odd coupling of Andrew Jackson and Martin Van Buren remade American politics in the late 1820s and 1830s. A wealthy Tennessee planter whose southern roots, early struggles with poverty, hot temper, and military heroism made him a popular icon, Jackson seemed to have little in common with Van Buren, whose career in New York politics and law trained him in the arts of organization and working with allies and enemies alike. In his two terms as president, Jackson strongly opposed South Carolina's nullification of a tariff that benefited northern industry, establishing his and his party's nationalist credentials and attracting northerners and many southerners dubious about South Carolina's willingness to disunite the United States. Jackson also blocked the rechartering of the Second Bank of the United States and federal aid for internal improvements, both crucial to promoters of nationalism and industry. As his chosen successor and a party manipulator, Van Buren continued Jackson's tradition of nationalism and limited government but without his color. Van Buren represented, as historian Richard Hofstadter wrote, "the placatory professional politician, whose leadership comes in large part out of his taste for political association, his liking for people, and his sportsman-like ability to experience political conflict without taking it as ground for personal rancor." In many ways, that described Lincoln, who attacked Van Buren on the stump but spent a pleasant evening with him, spinning stories.[6]

Jackson and his views also inspired another party. Starting out in 1828 as the National Republicans to distinguish themselves from the Democrats, they evolved into the Whigs. Taking their name from British opponents of King George III and aligning themselves with the colonists who waged the war for independence, they demonstrated their concerns about executive power in their criticism of "King Andrew." Henry Clay and Daniel Webster, the leaders of the American Whigs, reached different constituencies and inspired different loyalties. A Kentucky planter nicknamed "Harry of the West," Clay became a public darling for his down-to-earth oratory and the party's ideological leader for his "American System," a program of internal improvements to build roads and canals connecting regions and industries. A New Englander and a superior attorney and orator, Webster proved too much the old Federalist for many outside the Northeast and too corrupt and slippery for other party leaders.

While both preached nationalism and union, slavery demonstrated the contradictions in their ideologies and helped deprive them of the presidency. A slave owner who disliked slavery, Clay served as president of the American Colonization Society, an organization committed to returning slaves to Africa. Webster represented an antislavery region but saw no reason to shed blood, real or political, over the institution. For these and other reasons, Whigs found building a party difficult. Clay's economic program and moderate antislavery views vexed southerners, especially in the Deep South, where slavery predominated more than in the Upper South and the transportation provided by river networks limited interest in the American System.

Jackson's popularity also helped and hampered both parties. The Whigs, serving as the anti-Jackson party, attracted his opponents even after his death, with Democrats claiming to follow his example. Just as Democrats fed on Jackson and then his reputation, Whigs reacted to him and his legacy, but with more certainty about what they were against than about what they were for. In the South and the urban North, that legacy fostered obstacles for Whigs for whom Jackson loomed, dead or alive. John Calhoun of South Carolina broke with Jackson for a variety of reasons and might have led southern Whigs but disdained activist government, since that might promote antislavery legislation. John Tyler of Virginia agreed with Jackson on almost everything except his broad view of presidential power and bank veto, which made him a Whig in name but not in depth. Whigs owed a good deal of their support and ideology to the evangelical Protestantism of the Second Great Awakening, but the reforms blossoming from that movement limited their ability to attract new urban and immigrant voters who saw them as trying to impose their religious and social views on others. Those attitudes also struck voters as elitist, making Jackson's common-man appeal even more of a contrast to the Whigs.

Consequently, Whigs spent most of their existence just beyond the reach of power—and when they grasped it, it crumbled in their hands. In 1840, William Henry Harrison won the presidency when the party adopted the Jacksonians' approach, concentrating on slogans and nicknames like "Tippecanoe and Tyler Too." Indeed, Whigs learned their lesson so well that when a Democratic editor dismissed Harrison as an old farmer content with a "log cabin and hard cider," Whigs adopted the mantra and rode it to victory. But when Harrison died after a month in office, Tyler reverted to his Jacksonian ways, blocking Whig legislation and sowing dissension. In 1844, Clay came heartbreakingly close to defeating Democrat James Polk, but turning to another military hero in 1848 produced no better results: Zachary Taylor died in office after irking Whigs with his policies and patronage, and Millard Fillmore proved unable to unify the party. By 1852, the Whig party teetered on the brink of collapse, and the defeat that year of General Winfield Scott, its presidential candidate, almost sent it over the edge.

The Whigs' destruction resulted mainly from slavery and the social, economic, cultural, and political differences its presence bred. Northern and southern Whigs fought with one another and within their regions: across the North, conservative and antislavery Whigs struggled for power, while in the South, those willing to compromise with the North battled those committed to spreading and protecting slavery. Antislavery parties both gave and took away. In 1844, the Liberty Party diverted votes from Clay when he proved ambivalent about annexing Texas—but courting antislavery voters would have cost Clay support in the South. In 1848, the Free-Soil Party did more harm to Taylor's Democratic opponent, Lewis Cass, who advocated letting voters decide whether to permit slavery in new territory. Northerners resented bans on antislavery petitions in Congress and antislavery literature in southern mail, and Whigs bore much of the fallout: since Democrats already advocated states' rights and a limited federal government, on most issues they could more easily claim that their party would leave these matters up to states and individuals. The Whig tradition of reform and activism limited the party's ability to appeal to one section without offending the other, or even for its members in each section to agree with one another.

The Compromise of 1850 demonstrated the party system's fragility. Clay introduced the measures that ultimately formed the compromise: California statehood, a tougher fugitive slave law, a boundary dispute resolved for Texas and against New Mexico, the slave trade abolished in the District of Columbia, and territorial status for Utah and New Mexico with their citizens to vote on whether to allow slavery. When Clay's attempt to put them in one bill failed, Senator Stephen Douglas of Illinois broke them into individual bills, enabling senators to vote for or against each. However, uniting Democrats or northerners proved impossible, even for as shrewd a manipulator as Douglas. The battle over the compromise reflected regional differences, with northerners and southerners split and border state men generally providing the margins for passage. Further revealing Whig divisions, Taylor angered pro-compromise Whigs by vowing to veto the compromise. But after Taylor died on July 9, 1850, Fillmore lobbied for its passage and signed it, and Whigs either hailed or reviled Fillmore for his role in it. Democrats could sit back, enjoy the Whigs' civil war, and argue that their ideology of limited government and states' rights worked equally well, north or south. Meanwhile, Whigs found it impossible to unify the regions, and those of differing views within the regions, behind a more activist platform. In some areas, Whigs could win on local issues, but without a national, unified ideology, their demise was inevitable.

"Always a Whig in Politics"

That Abraham Lincoln became a Whig seems illogical. Son of a hard-scrabble farmer (a group traditionally more Jacksonian than Whig), Lincoln believed in free labor—that northerners could achieve economic independence and prosperity that slavery made unavailable to many southerners—and accordingly celebrated the farmer and his works. In Illinois, where Lincoln lived, anyone with ambitions beyond a local legislative or congressional district had more hope of satisfying them as a Democrat than as a Whig. While evangelical Protestantism contributed to the Whig Party's rise, Lincoln became a religious skeptic as a young man, tangled politically with noted Methodist minister Peter Cartwright, generally avoided formal religious ties, and had to wriggle free of accusations "that I am an open scoffer at Christianity." While Lincoln criticized reformers who put an issue above party loyalty, those reformers found Whigs more accommodating than Democrats and cost the Whigs support from less reform-minded voters.[7]

Instead, the party's proactive approach to affairs helped make Lincoln a devout Whig. Between his difficult relationship with his father and distaste for physical labor, Lincoln preferred to respect farmers from a distance and pursue a more cerebral line of work. As a boy, Lincoln enjoyed attention for his storytelling, which awoke him to the value of belonging to or even leading a group. Perhaps the Whigs attracted him because theirs was the party where others would take notice of him, one that emphasized the elite—even a meritocracy—over the leveling influence of the Democrats, among whom he would be just another in the crowd of farmers and small town strivers. Growing up in rural areas, he saw the value of good roads that connected farmers with their markets and became aware of Clay, a fellow Kentuckian, who advocated those roads. This awareness deepened when he married the daughter of one of Clay's political allies in Kentucky. Soon after moving to New Salem, Illinois, Lincoln ran for the legislature and explained his political principles: "Time and experience have verified to a demonstration, the public utility of internal improvements. That the poorest and most thinly populated counties would be greatly benefitted by the opening of good roads, and in the clearing of navigable streams within their limits, is what no person will deny." Losing in his first attempt, Lincoln spent four terms in the legislature and a term in Congress, as well as numerous campaigns, supporting Whig dogma.[8]

Indeed, Lincoln proved more loyal to the idea of party than did many other Whigs. From his arrival in New Salem, when he became close to a group of local rowdies who voted for him but not for other Whigs, he tried to broaden his party's appeal beyond the elites it attracted most easily. He even faced questions about his own connections when, after moving to Springfield, he wed Mary Todd, the daughter of a wealthy Kentucky Whig, prompting suspicions that he had left behind his old friends and threatening his political future. When Whigs supported some of their own office-seekers, including Clay and Taylor, grudgingly or not at all, Lincoln stayed with the party and justified their nominations or elections purely on pragmatic grounds both publicly and privately, saying in 1848, "Our only chance is with Taylor. I go for him, not because I think he would make a better president than Clay, but because I think he would make a better one than Polk, or Cass, or Buchanan, or any such creatures, one of whom is sure to be elected, if he is not."[9]

What Lincoln thought and did about slavery reflected his commitment to his party: political reality and his belief in the need for moderation tempered his hatred for the peculiar institution. Not for him the evangelical Protestant side of Whiggery or the tunnel vision of reformers: as he told the Young Men's Lyceum of Springfield in 1838, "Passion has helped us; but can do so no more. It will in future be our enemy. Reason, cold, calculating, unimpassioned reason, must furnish all the materials for our future support and defence." In his first public pronouncement on slavery—a legislative resolution he cowrote—he declared it "founded on both injustice and bad policy; but . . . the promulgation of abolition doctrines tends rather to increase than to abate its evils." While Congress could not "interfere with the institution of slavery in the different states," it could abolish it in Washington, D.C., if the people there approved of it. All of these stands reflected his abiding dislike for slavery and his pragmatism.[10]

During the 1840s, while Lincoln remained antislavery more in thought than in action, slavery mattered less to him than his party and profession did. As a lawyer, at different times he represented fugitive slaves and their masters. Lincoln visited the Kentucky plantations of the Todd family and his friend Joshua Speed, and in neither case did he offer significant objections to slaves serving him. After the 1844 election, he complimented an Illinois friend seeking unity between Whigs and the antislavery Liberty Party. "If the whig abolitionists of New York had voted with us last fall, Mr. Clay would now be president, whig principles in the ascendent, and Texas not annexed; whereas by the division, all that either had at stake in the contest, was lost," he said. "I never was much interested in the Texas question. . . . I never could very clearly see how the annexation would augment the evil of slavery. It always seemed to me that slaves would be taken there in about equal numbers, with or without annexation." Lincoln's comments suggested no interest in or awareness of the possibility of dividing Texas into several slave states, increasing southern power in Congress and on behalf of slavery—a more local or provincial view than the one held by more nationally minded Whig leaders, but the view of an antislavery party man concerned mainly with trying to win elections.[11]

Nevertheless, Lincoln subscribed to Whig doctrine, including that on slavery. During his House term, he joined other northern Whigs to support the Wilmot Proviso to bar slavery from territory acquired from Mexico. Exposed more to slavery—slave auctions went on near Capitol Hill—he tried to fashion a bill to end slavery in the District of Columbia but found northerners wary and southerners intransigent. When he returned to Illinois in 1849, his political career seemed over: Illinois Whigs rotated the one House seat they usually controlled, and the Democratic majority limited his chances of winning a statewide office like U.S. senator. Over the next five years, he participated little in politics, emerging most prominently to eulogize Clay when he died in 1852. Tellingly, Lincoln focused more on Clay's opinions about slavery than on his economic views, making the Whig leader more antislavery than his actions and policies suggested—a sign of Lincoln's interests and changes in the political landscape. Clay never felt that "the negroes were to be excepted from the human race. And yet Mr. Clay was the owner of slaves," Lincoln said. "Cast into life where slavery was already widely spread and deeply seated, he did not perceive, as I think no wise man has perceived, how it could be at *once* eradicated, without producing a greater evil, even to the cause of human liberty itself. His feeling and his judgment, therefore, ever led him to oppose both extremes of opinion on the subject."[12]

Clay's compromises demonstrated his—and Lincoln's—quest for an elusive middle ground, but that ground shifted radically less than two years after Clay's death. On January 4, 1854, Stephen Douglas introduced the Kansas-Nebraska Act, predicting to a southern colleague that it would cause "a hell of a storm." While Douglas spoke and acted far more bluntly and rambunctiously than Lincoln did, he topped even Lincoln's talent for understatement. Douglas advocated popular sovereignty, as a Democrat and in his legislation. Permitting voters to decide on slavery in the two territories required the Missouri Compromise's repeal, which he planned to do implicitly until southerners demanded that he do it explicitly. He did, winning support from southern Democrats and many southern Whigs, and President Franklin Pierce agreed to make the bill a party issue to keep northern Democrats in line. That proved unacceptable to antislavery Democrats, whom antislavery Whigs joined in opposition. The bill passed partly because southerners combined with "doughfaces"—a term apparently based on the premise that some northerners, like dough, lacked shape and color on the subject of slavery. In the process, the Kansas-Nebraska Act completed what the deaths of Clay and Webster, Pierce's lambasting of Winfield Scott in the 1852 election, new coalitions growing out of European immigration, and the rise of nativist and temperance political parties had begun and ultimately encouraged: the Whig Party's destruction.

The Kansas-Nebraska Act roused Lincoln from his political slumber for several reasons. For one, anything involving the "Little Giant" made him suspicious. Since coming to Springfield in the late 1830s,

Lincoln and Douglas had tangled politically. Lincoln saw Douglas as hiding behind claims of democracy in order to avoid a moral stand that might hurt him politically—and, worse, claiming in doing so to follow in the Founding Fathers' footsteps, which Lincoln found contemptible. Lincoln also opposed slavery and emotionalism. Douglas managed with one bill to bring both to the forefront, making the slavery debate noisier and violent. Beyond the ideological factors, on a less elevated or intellectual level, Lincoln the longtime political operator saw an opportunity to undercut Douglas and the Democrats and to benefit his party.

But which party? In 1854 and 1855, opponents of the Kansas-Nebraska Act began to coalesce in some places as a new party, the Republicans, while other Democrats and Whigs turned to the nativist American party, known as the Know-Nothings. While Lincoln refused to leave the Whigs as long as they at least gasped for breath, he also learned that old loyalties died slowly. In 1855, he sought a Senate seat from Illinois, but the legislature chose Lyman Trumbull when anti-Nebraska Democrats refused to vote for a Whig or anyone still claiming any connection to the party. As Lincoln told his old friend Speed in the summer of 1855, "I think I am a whig; but others say there are no whigs, and that I am an abolitionist. When I was at Washington I voted for the Wilmot Proviso as good as forty times, and I never heard of any one attempting to unwhig me for that. I now do no more than oppose the *extension* of slavery." Privately, to Speed, Lincoln criticized another political alternative more strongly than he did in public: "I am not a Know-Nothing. That is certain. How could I be? How can any one who abhors the oppression of negroes, be in favor of degrading classes of white people? Our progress in degeneracy appears to me to be pretty rapid."[13]

Lincoln eventually joined the Republicans out of necessity and choice. By 1855, the Whig Party was effectively dead, the Democrats had become prisoners of proslavery forces, and he found the Know-Nothings abhorrent. He needed a political home, since he believed too strongly in the importance of party and wanted too much to make a difference to remain on the outside looking in. Republicans often disagreed over how much to appeal to nativists in hopes of attracting Know-Nothings, their competition for the role of primary opponent of the Democrats. Although they battled over how strongly antislavery to be, Republicans joined together in opposing the spread of slavery into the territories and united for homesteads and internal improvements. That required no change in Lincoln, who had long since established his antislavery credentials and had experience in navigating between conservatives and reformers as a Whig.

Indeed, becoming a Republican gave Lincoln an opportunity for growth that the Whig Party never offered. He always viewed Whigs as seeking to improve society and encourage advancement. As a Republican, he would have the moral issue on which to peg these ideas. The importance of slavery enabled Lincoln to indulge and sharpen his political and oratorical talents and to help shape both his new party's direction and his approach to politics and policy. In 1854, responding to Douglas at Peoria, Illinois, he outlined the principles he attempted to follow for the rest of his career when he said that "as this subject is no other, than part and parcel of the larger general question of domestic slavery, I wish to MAKE and to KEEP the distinction between the EXISTING institution, and the EXTENSION of it, so broad, and so clear, that no honest man can misunderstand me, and no dishonest one, successfully misrepresent me."[14]

Unfortunately, misunderstanding and misrepresentation became hallmarks of the slavery debate in the late 1850s. It grew into a vicious circle: Republicans opposed its expansion and southerners demanded its growth and vilified its critics, prompting Republicans and even northerners unsympathetic to their views to attack southern society. In the North, Republicans struck a chord with voters. Whether on their own or in league with nativists, Republicans recorded an impressive string of victories throughout 1855 and 1856. Their first presidential candidate, John C. Frémont, ran far better than a first-time party and its standard bearer had any right to expect, carrying most of the North in losing in 1856 to Democrat James Buchanan, a Pennsylvanian who won the electoral college and the presidency mainly with southern support.

Proslavery violence helped the Republican cause. When the "Border Ruffians" tried to intimidate Kansans into accepting slavery, abolitionist John Brown and others responded by killing five proslavery settlers at the town of Pottawatomie. After Senator Charles Sumner of Massachusetts delivered a lengthy speech attacking slavery and its spread into Kansas and included gratuitous insults toward Senator Andrew Butler of South Carolina, Butler's cousin, Representative Preston Brooks, came onto the Senate floor and caned the abolitionist, whose injuries and trauma kept him from returning to the Senate for three years. Running as the Know-Nothing presidential candidate and conscious of the North's horror at the South's behavior, Fillmore complained, "Brooks' attack on Sumner has done more for Frémont than any 20 of his warmest friends . . . have been able to accomplish. . . . The Republicans ought to pension Brooks for life."[15]

The Great Debate, the Great Debates

What happened in Kansas and the Senate bothered Lincoln as exemplifying the radicalism and emotionalism that ran counter to his vision of how politics should operate. As both sides grew more rigid in their debates, Lincoln sharpened his comments on slavery—but not so sharply that he lost his talent for subtlety. In 1857, Chief Justice Roger Taney steered the Supreme Court to the *Dred Scott* decision, which denied that Congress could ban slavery from the territories—the heart of the Republican platform. A year later, at a party meeting, Lincoln referred to workmen erecting a building in order to explain what was essentially a slave power conspiracy. "We can not absolutely *know* that all these exact adaptations are the result of preconcert. But when we see a lot of framed timbers, different portions of which we know have been gotten out at different times and places and by different workmen—Stephen, Franklin, Roger and James, for instance," he said, "we find it impossible to not *believe* that Stephen and Franklin and Roger and James all understood one another from the beginning." In the same speech, Lincoln declared, "A house divided against itself cannot stand," softening the comment by noting that "I do not expect the Union to be *dissolved*—I do not expect the house to *fall*—but I *do* expect it will cease to be divided" and explaining the "tendency" toward the Union becoming a slave republic rather than a free one.[16]

Lincoln's comments reflected both party ideology and his political goals. To some Illinois Republicans, the "House Divided" speech opened him to charges of radicalism, which could have hurt his efforts to position himself as a moderate and to attract support from ex-Whigs less concerned about slavery. To Lincoln, his speeches reflected what he and many other Republicans saw as reality: a slave power determined to spread slavery into the North and maintain its control over government. Thus, workmen Stephen Douglas and Franklin Pierce and Roger Taney and James Buchanan did its bidding. More crucially, at the time of the "House Divided" speech, Illinois Republicans took the unprecedented step at their state convention of naming Lincoln their official opponent for Douglas, who was seeking a third term in the Senate but under a handicap. When intimidation and corruption forced through a proslavery constitution in Kansas, Buchanan went along. Douglas saw the lack of a legitimate vote in Kansas as corrupting the popular sovereignty he had championed. He broke with Buchanan, who deprived him of the usual party patronage and funding. In turn, some eastern Republicans, led by mercurial editor Horace Greeley, discussed supporting Douglas, reasoning that the enemy of their enemy could be their friend. "What does the New-York Tribune mean by it's constant eulogizing, and admiring, and magnifying [of] Douglas? Does it, in this speak the sentiments of the republicans at Washington?" Lincoln asked Lyman Trumbull. "Have they concluded that the republican cause generally, can be best promoted by sacrificing us here in Illinois? If so we would like to know it soon; it will save us a great deal of labor to surrender at once."[17]

By referring to conspiratorial workmen and divided houses, Lincoln hoped to remind Republicans that Douglas never belonged to the antislavery cause. In 1858, their seven debates in towns throughout Illinois gave him that chance. Professing not to care about slavery, just as long as voters decided the issue, Douglas appealed to prejudice and depicted Lincoln as advocating racial equality. Aware of the need for conservative votes and that Illinoisans limited black migration to their state, Lincoln tried to navigate between irreconcilable forces. He denied believing in even the possibility of racial equality, voting rights, or racial intermarriage. Yet he saw "no reason in the world why the negro is not entitled to all the natural rights enumerated in the Declaration of Independence," adding, "I agree with Judge Douglas he is not my equal in many respects—certainly not in color, perhaps not in moral and intellectual endowment. But in the right to eat the bread, without leave of anybody else, which his own hand earns, *he is my equal and the equal of Judge Douglas, and the equal of every living man.*"[18]

That election produced a pyrrhic victory for Douglas and a valuable loss for Lincoln. Lincoln won the popular vote, as measured by the election of new legislators, but Douglas won reelection thanks to holdovers from previous sessions and gerrymandering that benefited Democrats. During their second debate at Freeport, Lincoln asked Douglas a question that produced the answer for which Republicans hoped: popular sovereignty should continue to determine whether slavery would spread, not the *Dred Scott* decision. Douglas needed to make this point to win in Illinois and gain northern support, but it killed, or at least severely injured, his chances of winning southern support for any future presidential campaign. Not that the Freeport Doctrine offered anything original; Douglas had said it before. To say it again while running for the Senate, however, made it impossible for him to unsay it when he next sought the presidency.

For Lincoln, the race against Douglas cemented his importance as a state and national figure. As a Whig congressman, he drew little attention. Before turning Republican, he lost a bid for the Senate. Once he became a Republican, though, his star began to rise. At the 1856 convention, he won 110 votes for the vice presidential nomination— granted, mainly as the Illinois delegation's favorite son candidate, but it meant his name gained prominence in the party. In 1858, he took on the Democratic front-runner for the presidency, a two-term senator known for political cunning and for taking no prisoners in debate. Not only did Lincoln emerge largely unscathed, except for the unpleasant fact that he lost, but his side carried more votes than Douglas's. Lincoln had damaged Douglas's chances of winning the presidency in 1860 as a Democrat and probably eliminated any chance that he could run as a Republican. Indeed, to describe national politics after the Lincoln-Douglas election of 1858 as in a state of flux would be an understatement—and that fluidity would benefit Republicans who, like Lincoln, could avoid allowing uncertainty and possibility to divert them from their course.

TASTING A CANDIDACY

In November 1858, just after the vote assuring Stephen Douglas's reelection to the Senate, the *Gazette* of Lacon, Illinois, announced, "Abraham Lincoln for President in 1860." The next day, in Mansfield, Ohio, a Republican meeting made a similar pronouncement. These were small-town Republicans with little influence, but more prominent and powerful party members thought similarly. Lincoln's friend Jesse Fell, an Illinois businessman and politician, suggested that Lincoln might have presidential prospects. Lincoln allegedly replied, "Oh, Fell, what's the use of talking of me for the presidency whilst we have such men as Seward, Chase and others, who are so much better known to the people and whose names are so intimately associated with the principles of the Republican party." When Fell pressed him, Lincoln confessed, "I admit the force of much of what you say, and admit that I am ambitious, and would like to be President. I am not insensible to the compliment you pay me . . . but there is no such good luck in store of me as the presidency." A month later, when several Illinois Republicans met in Springfield and proposed endorsing him for president, Lincoln said no, and the other Republicans agreed: announcing too soon or seeming too ambitious would do more harm than good.[1]

Before long, though, Lincoln seemed to waver. In April 1859, he told an editor interested in promoting his candidacy, "I must, in candor, say I do not think myself fit for the Presidency. I certainly am flattered, and gratified, that some partial friends think of me in that connection; but I really think it best for our cause that no concerted effort, such as you suggest, be made"—without specifying how he considered himself unfit and whether he meant the Republican cause or his own nascent candidacy. While Lincoln's aura of diffidence reflected his political wisdom and realism, the Senate election clearly had changed his life. A *Chicago Press and Tribune* editor likened him to Lord Byron, who "woke up one morning and found himself famous," while David Davis, a circuit judge, friend, and fellow ex-Whig, told him that he now had "a national reputation."[2]

By April 1860, more conscious of his fame and reputation, Lincoln stuck his neck out further. "I will be entirely frank. The taste *is* in my mouth a little," he told Lyman Trumbull, the Republican senator from Illinois. As usual, when in the position of revealing his innermost thoughts, Lincoln managed not to be entirely frank. His law partner, William Herndon, captured two of Lincoln's most distinctive characteristics when he called him "the most shut-mouthed man" and his ambition "a little engine that knew no rest." Besides, other Republicans and several members of the opposition had drunk just as deeply at the well of presidential ambition, if not more so. For Lincoln to achieve his ambition would require the convergence of two points: that he put himself in a position to be nominated and that the other candidates fail. Ultimately, Lincoln succeeded by continuing to be a candidate after the 1858 election ended and conducting a campaign both brilliant and subtle. Meanwhile, the other candidates, sometimes considered brilliant or subtle or both, often proved to be neither.[3]

The Republican Field

Early in 1860, *Harper's Weekly* published an illustration based on photographs from Mathew Brady's studio. "Prominent Candidates for the Republican Presidential Nomination at Chicago" featured a rendering of still largely unbuilt, boggy Washington, D.C., and caricatures of eleven politicians who posed for the photographer. At the center sat William Henry Seward, in a portrait larger than the other ten, highlighting his status as front-runner. Equally appropriately, Seward tended to be at the center of what went on in his party, even if his ideology ranged toward what would now be considered the party's left or radical wing.[4]

Most candidates for the nomination considered Seward the man to beat. In contrast to Lincoln's humble beginnings, moodiness, and difficulties in getting ahead politically, Seward seemed to lead a charmed life. Born in 1801 and raised in an upper-middle-class family in upstate New York, he married the abolitionist daughter of a local judge whose estate became his own. Seward enjoyed reading the classics and tending his gardens, practiced law, and entered business—all more effortlessly than the Kentucky-born son of a yeoman farmer had done. Chance—a broken stagecoach wheel along a road—introduced Seward to Thurlow Weed, a newspaperman who helped him and became his closest friend. To call Weed his political manager understated how inseparable they were. Reportedly, Seward said, "Seward is Weed and Weed is Seward. What I do, Weed approves. What he says, I indorse. We are one." While Weed spoke for antislavery Whigs in the *Albany Evening Journal* and managed the legislature and local party leaders, Seward delivered carefully constructed, philosophical, at times blunt speeches. Both relied on their conviviality to win friends and placate potential enemies, displaying a rare ability to stand for principle, cut corners, and while away evenings with brandy, cigars, and friends, discussing everything from politics to literature.[5]

Seward's principled streak sometimes tried Weed's patience and created trouble for himself. Seward won two terms as governor (1839–42) but alienated nativists in New York and beyond by attacking anti-Catholic sentiment in public schools and proposing state support for parochial schools to help immigrants obtain an education. For his part, Weed shared Seward's opposition to anti-immigrant prejudice but considered the issue more politically than ideologically: swiping Irish votes from the opposition Democrats would boost Whig chances. Seward's position cost him votes in New York, and he and Weed avoided too much contact with the Know-Nothings as that party gained popularity during the 1850s. As the 1860 election approached, Seward's views figured to reap benefits with immigrant voters and cost him with former Know-Nothings.

Seward's position on African Americans similarly combined principle and shrewdness, simultaneously helping and hurting him politically. During the 1840s, as slavery increasingly resonated as a national issue, Seward made no effort to shade his views. When Virginia demanded the arrest of three black sailors who helped a fugitive slave escape to New York, Governor Seward replied that since New York had banned slavery, no crime had been committed, and he pushed laws through the legislature to block similar actions. Speaking in Cleveland, he assailed the fugitive slave law and prohibitions on black voting and jury service, concluding that slavery "*can* and *must* be abolished and you and I can and must do it." He volunteered to defend an insane black man who murdered four members of a white family, telling the jury, "I am the lawyer for society, for mankind, shocked beyond the power of expression, at the scene I have witnessed here of trying a maniac as a malefactor." The jury refused his attempt to send the killer to an insane asylum, and many of Seward's fellow residents of Auburn excoriated him.[6]

Nonetheless, his overall popularity, his thoughtfulness and principle mingled with conviviality, and Weed's astute management enabled Seward to overcome the controversies he caused or fanned. Twice he won election to the Senate, first in 1849 as part of a Whig Party split over slavery. He won again in 1855, still as a Whig but amid the party's disintegration and with the Know-Nothings gaining traction. More crucially, in 1855, Weed held together the antislavery troops while keeping Seward's opponents from uniting behind a challenger. Then, with Seward back in the Senate, they moved to the Republican Party and quickly accrued power there. The next year, Seward desperately wanted the party's first presidential nomination, and his prominence in antislavery circles meant that he could have had it for the asking. To Seward's chagrin, Weed held back, reasoning that the party would lose the first time out, possibly damaging his friend's reputation.

Indeed, Seward's antislavery views—with Weed's help—not only saved his reelection but also made him a political star. Trips to the South convinced him that the region had stagnated economically and culturally, heightening the need to keep slavery out of newly acquired lands if Americans hoped to achieve what Seward considered their imperial and economic destiny. Although he doubted the likelihood of racial harmony in the United States, even critics who questioned his commitment to the radical cause agreed that he displayed no racial prejudice, and supporters could accurately describe him as "embodying more distinctly than any other living man the Anti-Slavery sentiment of the Northern States." In his maiden major speech in the Senate, he attacked the Compromise of 1850, declaring, "We are not slaveholders. We cannot . . . be either true Christians or real freemen if we impose on another a chain that we defy all human power to fasten on ourselves" and that a "higher law than the Constitution" would stop the spread of slavery. In 1858, before a Republican gathering in Rochester, Seward described the debate over freedom and slavery as "an irrepressible conflict between opposing and enduring forces, and it means that the United States must and will, sooner or later, become either entirely a slaveholding nation, or entirely a free-labor nation."[7]

While winning him attention and a key role in shaping the Republican Party and its reputation, these sentiments created one of several political liabilities for him. By 1860, Seward seemed headed for the nomination, but his radicalism hamstrung his candidacy. First, the 1856 election highlighted the party's need to carry crucial states—Pennsylvania, Illinois, Indiana, and Ohio—where conservatives and Democrats held enough power to make an antislavery moderate a likelier vote-getter. Republicans also hoped to build support in border slave states—Kentucky, Missouri, Maryland, and Delaware—and perhaps even the upper South. Invoking a higher law and an irrepressible conflict thrilled antislavery northerners, but it made Seward anathema to others. And where Republicans already were popular—in New England and New York—he would add little to their prospects.

Oddly, given Weed's reputation for political legerdemain, he did Seward more harm than good in 1860. Their ties associated Seward with Weed's alleged use of bribery and involvement in swindles. After the numerous scandals that had plagued Democratic administrations, Republicans planned to attack corruption and promise clean government, but doing so would seem hypocritical with Seward atop the ticket. Seward and Weed also could be too clever for their own good. In 1859, when he should have been lining up support for the next year, Seward left the responsibility to Weed and took an eight-month European trip. Thinking that remaining in the country's political maelstrom might harm Seward's chances, Weed deemed it best to remove his friend from the line of political fire. Instead, Seward's absence reduced his public presence and limited his ability to address criticism. Then, upon his return, he and Weed agreed on the need to moderate his image. Seward delivered a Senate speech reassuring the South that he and his party would leave slavery alone in that region, denying significant sectional differences and redefining regional differences as the "capital states" of the South and the "free labor" states of the North. Instead of creating the appearance of moderation, the speech made radicals already uncertain of his loyalty and rectitude all the queasier while doing nothing to assuage moderate and conservative displeasure with him.[8]

Seward faced another important and unlikely obstacle to the nomination: Horace Greeley. In 1838, Greeley began both a newspaper and, with Seward and Weed, an alliance—they called it a political firm. The three worked well together, and Greeley's *New York Tribune* became a major Whig organ. Then, after the 1854 election, Greeley wrote a letter dissolving the partnership, complaining that despite his labors, loyalty, and personal and financial needs and sacrifices, Weed ignored his desire for office. From Weed's perspective, Greeley's quirky personality, love for reform movements great and small, and bouts with what may have been depression made him an unsupportable candidate for office. But Weed had promoted Greeley's protégé-turned-enemy Henry Raymond, the cofounder of the *New York Times*, for office, because Weed needed a more conservative voice on the party ticket and Raymond lacked Greeley's independent bent. By early 1860, Greeley resolved to block Seward's nomination, for the logical reason that he doubted his chances of victory and for the personal reasons that he would avenge earlier slights, outmaneuver Weed, and possibly set himself up for political office.

Greeley alone was formidable, but others felt similarly about Seward. In New York, some radical Republicans doubted Seward's fealty to their antislavery views, including *New York Evening Post* editor William Cullen Bryant, a Democrat until that party's southern leanings drove him away. Ex-Democrats like him disagreed with former Whigs on such issues as internal improvements and tariffs, adding to Seward's problems. Republicans shared a unifying ideology of freedom, but the speed with which that freedom should come to slaves divided them, as did other issues. Some old Democrats and Whigs overcame those divisions or deemed them too minor to divert their new party from a greater cause.

Other Republicans wanted anyone but Seward, but the alternatives, in political discussions and the *Harper's* illustration, had their own problems. The most frequently mentioned possibility, Salmon Portland Chase, differed from Seward personally and politically. Born in 1808, Chase had left his native New Hampshire before his tenth birthday when his father's death left his family destitute. Chase studied with his uncle, Ohio's Episcopal bishop, who expected his nephew to work hard, study hard, and have as little fun as possible. Eventually, Chase started a school in Washington, D.C., and just as exposure to his wife's wealthier family and Weed's political shrewdness shaped Seward, Chase entered the orbit of William Wirt, the attorney general in John Quincy Adams's cabinet, inspiring him to pursue a career in law. Chase did so in Ohio, where he found great professional success and entered politics, in part to ease the pain of his personal life: he married three times, and each wife died, leaving him to raise two daughters. Even before those events, he displayed little of the enjoyment that Seward derived from politics, philosophical discussions, or small talk, or the sense of humor that Lincoln developed amid his own personal pain. Chase never learned how to laugh or make others laugh, and it damaged his political career. His piety helped him steer clear of the corruption allegations that plagued Seward, but it also meant that when he acted in his own interest, his efforts to justify himself could be clumsy and annoying, rooted in his belief that whatever he did, the higher cause for which he did it justified the political benefits he received and kept others from gaining.

Yet Seward and Chase became allies and friends out of a shared belief in social uplift, especially by fighting slavery. Just as Seward took principled stands, Chase challenged a mob that was out to tar and feather abolitionist James Birney in 1836. Thus began Chase's long fight for freedom, speaking and writing against the spread of slavery, representing fugitive slaves, and leading efforts to turn foes of slavery into a political force. "The Constitution found slavery and left it a state institution—the creature and dependent of State law—wholly local in its existence and character," he argued, and the Fifth Amendment ban on Congress depriving any "person" of "life, liberty, or property without due process of law" prohibited the federal government from extending or protecting slavery. Chase took his arguments to the Supreme Court, where Seward became his co-counsel in one case. The two agreed on the need to attack slavery through the political process and began corresponding. Chase hoped Seward would join the Free-Soilers in 1848, but Seward insisted that the two-party system with the Whigs in it provided the best means to combat slavery.[9]

Chase differed from Seward in other ways that hampered his presidential hopes. Seward deferred to Weed, but Chase had no true manager or close advisers (at least, none he would listen to) and became too involved in his campaigns when politicians were supposed to appear aloof. While Seward remained a loyal Whig, Chase had been an antislavery Democrat but lacked a cadre of Democrats-turned-Republicans to support him. More critically, in 1849, he won a Senate seat by making a deal to eliminate some anti-black legislation in Ohio, but at the political expense of other Free-Soilers and especially antislavery Whigs who never forgave him. Then, as a Republican, he won Ohio's governorship in 1855 by maneuvering with Know-Nothings. While he hoped to advance the antislavery cause and limit nativist influence, he benefited politically and worked with a group that Seward and Lincoln refused to join. Chase's opponents saw these elections as examples of his excessive ambition and inability to distinguish between himself and a cause and planned to make him pay for it later. While Seward could use charm to assuage such feelings, Chase's certitude and rectitude put off potential allies and kept him from understanding why. Nor did it help that Chase declined an invitation to speak in New York City before a group seeking alternatives to Seward—but Lincoln accepted and at Cooper Union delivered one of his greatest speeches.

Even more important, moderate and conservative Republicans saw Seward and Chase as different sides of the same radical coin. As Carl Schurz, a Seward supporter and a German immigrant influential in that voting bloc, told Chase, if Republicans "have courage enough to nominate an advanced antislavery man, they will nominate Seward, if not, they will not nominate you." Moderates and especially conservatives sought a less radical or overtly ambitious candidate than Seward or Chase, with views more compatible with their own. That created a boomlet for Missourian Edward Bates, an old—literally, for that time, at age sixty-six—Whig, so conservative that he had never joined the Republican Party. Nonetheless, he appealed to ex-Whigs as one of them and for delivering a major speech in favor of internal improvements at a convention in 1847 on rivers and harbors that stamped him as a potential leader. Also, despite living in a border slave state, Bates had antislavery credentials: he had emancipated his slaves, opposed the Mexican-American War as an effort to extend slavery into new territories and thereby harm white migrants, and supported the Wilmot Proviso.[10]

Bates also benefited from geography and aid from an unlikely team: Greeley, the reformist ex-Whig, and Francis Preston Blair, an old Jacksonian Democrat and hardheaded political operative who usually opposed whatever Greeley and Bates supported. But Greeley wanted a candidate to derail Seward and thought a border state politician would attract more votes than a northerner. Greeley had the means to serve his cause through the *Tribune*'s daily and popular weekly editions, and Blair had the political savvy and managerial experience that Greeley lacked. Their journalism backgrounds and shared distaste for Seward gave them an affinity that helped overcome old differences. Also, Blair was Virginia-born and Kentucky-bred, lived in Maryland, and had a son in Missouri, giving him a better sense than most other Republicans of how to win the border states. As one Blair ally wrote, "We Republicans in Missouri, who are placed politically on the border, and where the fight is literally face to face with the lawless National Democracy, regard it as a matter of great natural advantage that the Republican party can select a reliable and able leader from a Slaveholding State."[11]

Unfortunately for his supporters, Bates had avoided politics for decades, helping and hindering him. At a time when the office supposedly sought the man, he escaped the appearances of corruption and ambition that plagued Seward and Chase, and being out of the limelight reduced his opportunities to make enemies who might seek revenge later, as Seward and Chase would discover. But Bates's Whiggery and early distaste for the Republican Party posed a problem. In 1856, he backed Millard Fillmore's Know-Nothing candidacy. While Bates reacted more as the Whig he had been than as a nativist, the important German-American constituency might abandon Republicans if they chose Bates. Further, while Seward disappeared to Europe and Chase sat in a crucial state, Bates never traveled from his home in a border slave state off the beaten Republican path, keeping him from meeting potential supporters. When he addressed issues in a public questionnaire, he sought to reassure immigrants and endorsed colonizing ex-slaves in Africa and Central America, as well as a transcontinental railroad and a homestead act. This pleased Republicans, but his potential border state voters lambasted him, possibly driving a stake through the best argument for his nomination—the support he might win in his home region—though Greeley and Blair continued to hope and plot.

Republicans also could turn to another aged candidate with border state appeal: John McLean. A seventy-five-year-old Ohioan, McLean came to the Supreme Court in 1829 as an appointee of John Quincy Adams, whom he served as postmaster general and who concluded that McLean "thinks of nothing but the Presidency by day and dreams of nothing else by night." Throughout his career, McLean switched parties whenever he thought it would benefit his chances for a nomination. He pushed for a decision in the *Dred Scott* case in 1856, hoping to use his dissent as a platform from which to seek the Republican nomination. Even if McLean had little chance, his moderation, political gymnastics, and experience could have helped him, especially in a divided convention, and his Ohio background might have split that state's delegation, harming Chase's chances.[12]

Similarly suspect but with conservative appeal, Simon Cameron came from Pennsylvania, making him a possibility if Republicans found no other way to win that swing state. He opposed slavery, but not so much that it kept him from working with proslavery forces. Like McLean, he jumped parties whenever it improved his prospects. Worse, while Seward's ties to Weed gave him a whiff of corruption, Cameron created a discernible odor. He had been a political boss long enough to reveal managerial talent, become rich, and leave a trail of accusations in his wake. Nicknames like Andrew Jackson's "Old Hickory" could benefit a politician, but Cameron's reminded voters of his dubious past: "The Great Winnebago Chief," which he earned by going to present-day Minnesota to negotiate a treaty with a tribe to obtain land for the federal government and paying them in scrip that could be cashed only at a bank he owned in Pennsylvania.

While McLean and Cameron were long shots, most of the others caricatured in *Harper's* were even longer shots. John Bell should not have been included, since he was neither a Republican nor antislavery. John Frémont had had his chance in 1856, and no major Republicans showed interest in a rerun. Besides, none of his problems had gone away: limited political experience, rumors of corruption, and untrue but damaging allegations that he belonged to the Catholic church. Another of those depicted, Cassius M. Clay, was a Kentuckian, but his abolitionism put him at the radical end of the party when Republicans agreed on the need for moderate votes. The still Whiggish William Pennington of New Jersey had gained notoriety by becoming Speaker of the House in December 1859 but as a compromise choice for his lack of controversy and fame, not for his importance or influence. Nathaniel Banks had been Speaker of the House and governor of Massachusetts, both critical posts, but Republicans had no need to solidify their already strong New England support. He also dallied enough with nativists to make him anathema to the German-American constituency, if they thought of him at all as a candidate, and in a neat irony that nativists were unlikely to enjoy, he pledged his support to Seward.

Other Republicans whom *Harper's* ignored either had hopes or appealed to Republicans in their states. William L. Dayton had been Frémont's running mate in 1856, and some in New Jersey hoped to elevate him, never stopping to consider that the distant runner-up for Dayton's spot four years before had been Lincoln. Among Ohio Republicans, radicals, especially onetime Whigs, preferred Benjamin Wade, a U.S. senator, but that further split the state's delegation, which already had divided between Chase and McLean.

The artist who used Brady's renderings may have intended nothing in how he positioned everyone but Seward. Chase and McLean flanked the New Yorker, with Bates above him on one side, possibly signifying their importance, except that Banks sat opposite Bates on Seward's other side and realistically had no chance unless lightning struck. Below Seward sat Lincoln, appropriately located: to his right and in proximity but largely under the radar.

The Self-Made Man

In an essay on Lincoln, historian Richard Hofstadter argues that he exemplified the image of "the self-made man," the popular ideal of the poor boy or young man pulling himself up in society on his own. Although cynical about Lincoln, Hofstadter has proved to be both right and wrong. Perhaps more than any other candidate in his time, Lincoln engineered his nomination, or the steps that made it possible, without leaving fingerprints. Another way to describe Lincoln might be to call him the self-contained man: his control over himself and his ability to control others through subtle manipulation made his success possible. Granted, knowing the result adds to the luster of Lincoln's wisdom, but anyone with political knowledge and the opportunity to be his shadow in 1859 and early 1860 should have been able to see how shrewdly he acted, especially in comparison with his main opponents.[13]

First, Lincoln sought to keep Republicans inside and outside of Illinois focused on their survival rather than on Stephen Douglas's charms. Indeed, his concerns reveal a deeper commitment to his party's antislavery ideology than that held by others exalted for their fidelity to the principles of freedom and willing to join forces with Douglas, whose opposition to the slave power and Buchanan rested on different grounds from theirs. In 1858, Lincoln complained to Lyman Trumbull about eastern Republicans, especially Greeley, who seemed to support Douglas against him. "All dallying with Douglas by Republicans," he warned, "is, at the very least, time, and labor lost." He told Kansas Republicans that "the only danger will be the temptation to lower the Republican Standard in order to gather recruits." To a onetime Illinois legislator, Lincoln observed, "Douglas managed to be supported both as the best means to *break down*, and to *uphold* the slave power. No ingenuity can long keep those opposing elements in harmony." Lincoln warned of a fight over "whether the Republican party can maintain its identity, or be broken up to form the tail of Douglas' new kite."[14]

Lincoln worried about Republicans lurching too far toward conservatism, as represented by Douglas's willingness to abide slavery, but he fretted as much about party members ranging toward abolitionism. As Lincoln knew from the controversy over his "House Divided" speech and the conservatives who backed Douglas over him in 1858, radical Republicans could drive moderates and conservatives to Douglas or to some other waiting politician. He warned Chase and other Ohioans against opposing the Fugitive Slave Act's constitutionality and advised Representative Schuyler Colfax of Indiana "to hedge against divisions in the Republican ranks generally" in that state, all of which kept his name before other party leaders.[15]

More important, Lincoln made it a point to spend the political off-year of 1859 in the public eye. Historian Don E. Fehrenbacher calls it "his year of self-discovery," but he could have called it the year in which Lincoln's party and country really began to discover him. After the 1858 election, Lincoln told his friend Dr. Anson Henry, "I am glad I made the late race. It gave me a hearing on the great and durable question of the age, which I could have had in no other way. . . . I believe I have made some marks which will tell for the cause of civil liberty long after I am gone." No sooner did he tell Henry that he expected to "sink out of view" than he set out to be remembered, beginning work on a book version of the debates—two months after Republicans met to discuss his presidential prospects and four months after the 1858 election brought him so much notice. Such a book might help him reach audiences who had neither been present for his exchanges with Douglas nor read about them in the press—and would be an authoritative version. By the time it came out, the

Republican National Convention was about to begin, and the book may have enhanced his profile among the delegates.[16]

Lincoln also confronted the issue of nativism, subtly and publicly. Theodore Canisius, a German-language newspaper editor in Illinois and recipient of funding from Lincoln, sought Lincoln's view of a Massachusetts law restricting the voting rights of naturalized citizens. Although disgusted by anti-immigrant sentiment, Lincoln had carefully avoided offending nativists. Replying to his supporter, he disclaimed any right to tell another state what to do, befitting his party's response to slavery. But he captured the problem of linking Republican and nativist ideology when he wrote, "Understanding the spirit of our institutions to aim at the *elevation* of men, I am opposed to whatever tends to *degrade* them. I have some little notoriety for commiserating the oppressed condition of the negro; and I should be strangely inconsistent if I could favor any project for curtailing the existing rights of *white men*, even though born in different lands, and speaking different languages from myself." He also would accept unity with Know-Nothings, he said, "if it can be had on republican grounds; and I am not for it on any other terms."[17]

Although financially obliged to concentrate on his law practice, which suffered during his campaign, Lincoln stayed before the public. He accepted speaking engagements in several states and found other ways to make his presence felt. Unable to attend a celebration of Thomas Jefferson's birthday in Boston, he sent a letter lauding the Declaration of Independence and its author and described Republican fidelity to Jefferson's principles as stronger than that of the Democrats who claimed his mantle. "The democracy of to-day hold the *liberty* of one man to be absolutely nothing, when in conflict with another man's right of *property*," he wrote. "Republicans, on the contrary, are for both the *man* and the *dollar*; but in cases of conflict, the man *before* the dollar." Happily for Lincoln and his future, Bostonians and Republican editors elsewhere liked and praised his words.[18]

Perhaps not coincidentally, Lincoln's travels took him to places where he could appeal to Republican convention delegates: Ohio, Wisconsin, Indiana, Iowa, and Kansas Territory, covering four thousand miles and twenty-three speeches. Then, in 1860, he spoke in New York and New England, where his name recognition paled in comparison with Seward's and Chase's. Thus, while other candidates stayed out of view—Seward in Europe, others in their home states—Lincoln acted in his own interests without violating taboos by campaigning openly.

What Lincoln said proved as important as where he said it. Conscious of his old opponent's status as Democratic front-runner and of a recent *Harper's* article in which Douglas tried to justify putting slavery in the territories to a vote, Lincoln mocked Douglas's oratorical and literary style, "gu-reat per-inciple" of popular sovereignty, and "explanations explanatory of explanations explained." Since Douglas had long played Moby Dick to Lincoln's Captain Ahab—ideally, for Lincoln's purposes, with better results—concentrating on the Little Giant seemed in character. Also, with some Republicans pondering Douglas in 1858 and the Little Giant's strained relations with Buchanan, Lincoln may have been trying to convince Republicans outside of Illinois and to reassure himself that other antislavery politicians would never accept his longtime rival. By targeting Douglas, Lincoln subtly reminded voters that no candidate had more experience battling him—and, in 1858, with a modicum of success. With fewer radical statements to explain than those of Seward or Chase, and without the conservative views that Bates sought to overcome with newfound Republicanism, Lincoln followed his instincts and staked out the middle. In Columbus, where Ohio Republicans could choose between the conservative McLean and radicals Chase and Wade, Lincoln described their party's "chief and real purpose," which critics saw as radical, as "eminently conservative. It proposes nothing save and except to restore this government to its original tone in regard to this element of slavery, and there to maintain it, looking for no further change, in reference to it, than that which the original framers of the government themselves expected and looked forward to."[19]

Lincoln also had the valuable talent of knowing how to tailor his comments to his audience. In Cincinnati, where some Kentuckians would cross the Ohio River to listen to him, he took the unusual step of addressing the crowd as if it consisted entirely of southerners and Douglas Democrats—a different approach, but one that those present could appreciate, since they dealt regularly with Lincoln's opposition. This gave Lincoln the opportunity to reassure his listeners of his moderate views and commitment to Republican principles: he had no desire to interfere with slavery where it existed and understood the South's concerns but steadfastly supported the Union. "If there was a necessary conflict between the white man and the negro, I should be for the white man as much as Judge Douglas; but I say there is no such necessary conflict," he told his listeners before trying to balance his position between antislavery and free labor. "I say that there is room enough for us all to be free, and that it not only does not wrong the white man that the negro should be free, but it positively wrongs the mass of the white men that the negro should be enslaved; that the mass of white men are really injured by the effect of slave labor in the vicinity of the fields of their own labor." He also invoked several Founding Fathers—each a slave owner—when he said, "We mean to treat you as near as we possibly can, like Washington, Jefferson and Madison treated you. We mean to leave you alone, and in no way to interfere with your institution."[20]

In addition to similar comments at speeches in two Wisconsin towns, Lincoln made it a point to praise free labor before audiences in Ohio and Indiana and an agricultural group in Wisconsin. In the process, he merged ostensibly nonpartisan purposes with an appeal to a key component of Republican ideology. He reminded Indianapolis listeners that he had been a hired laborer in his youth and never considered himself worse off than a slave, as some critics of Republicans tried to suggest. In Wisconsin, he hailed "*free* labor—the just and generous, and prosperous system, which opens the way for all—gives hope to all, and energy, and progress, and improvement of condition to all." These comments could appeal to any northerner—and pointed out that Douglas and other Democrats allowed southerners opposed to free labor to dictate their party's positions and might remain loyal to those southerners if Republicans worked too closely with the Little Giant and his followers.[21]

When Lincoln veered into Kansas shortly before a territorial election, he refined his message to reach that audience. With John Brown attacking Harpers Ferry shortly before his arrival, Lincoln condemned violence, reaching out to Kansans weary of continually fighting over slavery and conscious of Brown's role in their own battles. In "Bleeding Kansas," Lincoln argued against the wisdom of popular sovereignty differently than in other places. Addressing Kansans directly, he said, "You have, at last, at the end of all this difficulty, attained what we, in the old North-western Territory, attained without any difficulty at all. Compare, or rather contrast, the actual working of this new policy with that of the old, and say whether, after all, the old way—the way adopted by Washington and his compeers—was not the better way." Kansans could understand him perfectly.[22]

Nowhere did Lincoln demonstrate his understanding of his audience more than in his first speech in New York City, delivered late in February 1860 at the Cooper Union. Invited to speak at abolitionist minister Henry Ward Beecher's Plymouth Church in Brooklyn, he wound up at the Cooper Union when his hosts relocated the event. There, Republicans seeking an opponent for Seward sponsored a lecture series featuring prominent Republicans—but not Chase, who declined to come, or Bates, whom they never invited. Whether the committee invited Lincoln to scout him or simply to import another antislavery politician who might remind New Yorkers that someone other than Seward could criticize the institution is uncertain. Nor is it certain whether Lincoln thought of this as a step on the road to a possible nomination or as just an opportunity to reach a new audience and find an excuse for a trip east to visit his son, going to school in New England. But less than two months before, Lincoln had met with several Republican allies, who had wanted to start working for his nomination as president, and he had approved their efforts. Even if he still doubted his chances, he knew that others were at work on his behalf, and he had taken steps in the same direction.

That night at Cooper Union, he knew that he was a candidate, and thus he knew the stakes. Whatever his motivations for coming or those of his hosts for inviting him, Lincoln grasped that a New York audience would be more sophisticated and accustomed to political and literary oratory than most Ohioans or Kansans, that his invitation grew out of more than a mere desire to hear him discourse on political issues, and that looking and sounding too western and rural would hurt him with his audience. Thus, he bought a new suit and prepared more carefully for this talk than any other he had ever delivered. Not only did he impress New Yorkers with his learning and logic, but he did so in front of Horace Greeley and William Cullen Bryant. Whether or not they evaluated him as a candidate, they were key opinion makers who could help his national standing. Lincoln scholar Harold Holzer has called it "the speech that made Lincoln president," and while other events intervened, that night at Cooper Union certainly planted important seeds.[23]

At Cooper Union, Lincoln combined not only the old and the new but also the historian and the pragmatic ideologue. As usual, he targeted Douglas. He began with the Little Giant's premise about the expansion of slavery: "Our fathers, when they framed the Government under which we live, understood this question just as well, and even better, than we do now." Lincoln announced, "I fully indorse this," then explained why: his research, footnoted throughout his speech, showed that the Framers opposed the institution's spread. Thus, he called Douglas a liar without using the term but by relying on facts and logic. Lincoln asked southerners who accused Republicans of violating George Washington's warnings against sectional parties in his Farewell Address, "Could Washington himself speak, would he cast the blame of that sectionalism upon us, who sustain his policy, or upon you, who repudiate it?" Similarly, he defied them to prove Republican involvement in Harpers Ferry or in promoting slave insurrections. Thus, Republicans—indeed, any northerner—faced an impossible task: "The question recurs, what will satisfy them? Simply this: We must not only let them alone, but we must, somehow, convince them that we do let them alone." What would convince southerners? "This, and this only: cease to call slavery *wrong*, and join them in calling it *right*. And this must be done thoroughly—done in *acts* as well as in *words*. Silence will not be tolerated—we must place ourselves avowedly with them." His conclusion drew roars of applause—appropriately, because he came as close as he ever did to roaring, even using moderate language and concentrating as much on what Douglas claimed about the Framers as on what southerners claimed about the Framers and themselves:

"Let us be diverted by none of these sophistical contrivances . . . such as Union appeals beseeching true Union men to yield to Disunionists, reversing the divine rule, and calling, not the sinners, but the righteous to repentance—such as invocations to Washington, imploring men to unsay what Washington said, and undo what Washington did."[24]

While the Cooper Union speech paid dividends, Lincoln was proactive in other key ways. Using skills honed over a quarter of a century in Whig and Republican politics, he kept the diverse group that made up the Illinois Republican Party behind him. In doing so, he distinguished himself from competing candidates: Chase, who fumbled efforts to line up Ohio Republicans unanimously or sat back and expected others to follow him; Bates, who maintained a dignified distance or mangled his attempt to involve himself; Seward, who left matters up to Weed, who had to overcome longstanding differences between old Whig factions that had continued in the Republican Party; and other aspirants who simply hoped to enter the convention as their state's favorite son and wait for lightning to strike.

Not that Lincoln's quest for unity was easy. When he had sought a Senate seat in 1855, he had support from Whigs like David Davis, the judge before whom he appeared on the legal circuit, and Lincoln's old party correctly blamed his loss to Lyman Trumbull on antislavery Democrats like Norman Judd, a longtime legislator who went on to chair the Republican state committee. Even after becoming Republicans, ex-Whigs still feuded with former Democrats, but not over Lincoln—except over which of them revered him more.

In an era in which state delegations often nominated or at least bowed toward favorite sons at national party conventions, Lincoln benefited instead of Trumbull, who defeated him for the Senate in 1855. How Trumbull, then more highly regarded and nationally prominent, wound up on the sidelines also demonstrated Lincoln's sagacity. Trumbull's election had come before the Illinois Republican Party officially existed, but the divisions that propelled him to the Senate survived among Republicans. While Trumbull felt that John McLean might draw diverse support, perhaps because the *Chicago Press and Tribune* suggested them as a ticket, Lincoln made it a point to keep discussing politics with him and assure him of his support for reelection. In turn, Trumbull reported on Republican Chicago mayor Long John Wentworth's efforts to drive wedges between ex-Democrats like himself and ex-Whigs like Lincoln, who advised caution. "You better write no letters which can possibly be distorted into opposition, or quasi opposition to me. There are men on the constant watch for such things out of which to prejudice my peculiar friends against you," Lincoln wrote. "While I have no more suspicion of you than I have of my best friend living, I am kept in a constant struggle against suggestions of this sort. I have hesitated some to write this paragraph, lest you should suspect I do it for my own benefit, and not for yours; but on reflection I conclude you will not suspect me." Accordingly, Trumbull told his supporters to keep his name out of the presidential discussion.[25]

How Lincoln dealt with these people on an individual level proved crucial to his success in 1860. Lincoln cherished his friends but revealed himself fully to none of them, with the exception of Joshua Speed, to whom he had been close in the 1830s and early 1840s but who had long since moved to Kentucky. This suggests the degree to which Lincoln controlled his emotions, enabling him to make hard decisions about his political future without basing them on the advice of—or impact on—one friend only. In this way, he avoided depending too much on one person, in contrast to Seward and Weed, or only on himself, as Chase did. Thus, Davis and Judd carped about each other face-to-face or in letters but remained focused on Lincoln. In turn, he retained control of his political life and could agree and act with either man according to what best suited him. Each had friends and enemies, but a variety of Illinois Republicans worked on Lincoln's behalf. Indeed, his handling of this constellation of political talent foreshadowed how he managed his cabinet—and just as he managed that group masterfully during the Civil War, he harnessed Illinoisans for his nomination. What William Herndon said of his early life in New Salem proved true later: "He always had influential and financial friends to help him; they almost fought each other for the privilege of assisting Lincoln." More crucially, Lincoln knew how to use their assistance and when to ignore it.[26]

Judd's role underscores Lincoln's shrewdness and, when necessary, selfishness. Backing Trumbull in 1855 cost Judd dearly with Lincoln's friends—the election had been so bitter that Mary Todd Lincoln ended her long friendship with Julia Jayne Trumbull and branded Judd an enemy for life. Judd's other problems included debts he incurred for the party in managing it during Lincoln's Senate campaign in 1858 and a feud with Wentworth, a Chicago publisher and the loosest editorial cannon west of Horace Greeley. Lincoln helped Judd with the debts, endorsed him to Chicago businessmen, and backed him through intermediaries without offending the mercurial Wentworth enough to turn him into an enemy.

In turn, sticking by Judd paid huge dividends. First, fearing that Illinois Republicans might veer toward other candidates, Lincoln urged Judd to take action. In October 1859, a *Chicago Press and Tribune* editor, Joseph Medill, had trumpeted Lincoln to a Pennsylvania Republican: "He can carry the entire Northwest—Ind. included. He . . . was an old Clay Whig, is right on the tariff and he is exactly right on all other issues. Is there any man who could suit Pennsylvania better[?] The West is entitled to the president and he lives in the very heart of it." Judd apparently used his friendship with Medill and other *Press and Tribune* editors to make sure those sentiments appeared more often in print.[27]

Judd did far more for Lincoln outside of Illinois. When Judd went to New York in December 1859 for a Republican National Committee meeting, Lincoln wrote to him, "I find some of our friends here, attach more consequence in getting the National convention into our State than I did, or do. Some of them made me promise to say so to you." By reporting this desire and urging Judd to push to hold the convention after Democrats met, Lincoln may have managed subtly to give an order that Judd would consider his own idea. If he accomplished this, the letter suggested, Judd might please party allies and foes working on Lincoln's behalf.[28]

Crucially for Lincoln, Judd delivered. Before the committee, he emphasized Chicago's central location and ample railroads and hotels while shooting down other sites where Lincoln's opponents could stack the spectator stands. Judd also positioned himself to use his influence around town to make more Republicans more comfortable and fill the galleries for Lincoln. The committee had split between Chicago and St. Louis, and the latter would benefit Bates. Ultimately, the committee voted eleven to ten for Chicago, meaning Judd cast the deciding vote. Judd and other allies proved to be more than puppets, but Lincoln's string-pulling clearly demonstrated his abilities as a puppeteer with living subjects.

Not that Lincoln would have admitted it, since doing so would have been unseemly and egotistical. While Lincoln had ample self-confidence—running for the legislature at age twenty-three gave an early sign of it, and his political pursuits exemplified it—he was modest and self-deprecating. Still convinced of Lincoln's presidential prospects, Jesse Fell pushed him to prepare a campaign autobiography late in 1859, a year after their first conversation about running for the office. Lincoln produced a brief account, explaining that "there is not much of it, for the reason, I suppose, that there is not much of me." The material appeared first in a small Pennsylvania newspaper but gained wide distribution. Republicans were beginning to get to know Lincoln and at just the right time.[29]

The Opposition

In normal circumstances, Lincoln's suggestion that Republicans hold their convention after Democrats met would have been shrewd—all the better to know the Democratic choice. In retrospect, it looks even better. Democrats had far worse problems than those confronting Republicans in 1860. One Democrat loomed above all others as a possible standard-bearer but with one major difficulty: his views and those of most of his party had diverged too far for his Democratic opponents to reconcile themselves to supporting him.

Stephen Douglas had many reasons to expect his third try for the Democratic nomination to be the charm. In 1852, he had joined a large field but ruined his chances: only thirty-nine, he had acted with the impulsiveness of youth, choosing a running mate before the convention and underwriting a newspaper whose editors assaulted his main opponents. Those actions turned off Democrats already divided so badly that they required forty-nine ballots to settle on a comparative nonentity, Franklin Pierce. By the end of Pierce's term, Douglas had established himself as a Democratic power, but doing so through the Kansas-Nebraska Act might have relegated him to the status of such Senate luminaries as Henry Clay, Daniel Webster, and John Calhoun. Their impressive and controversial careers made them alternately loved and feared, respected and hated—in other words, too controversial to be nominated or, if nominated, elected president. Thus, in 1856, Democrats chose the reliably conservative and uncontroversial James Buchanan. Still young enough to wait, Douglas could have bided his time, but he broke with the president: not only did Buchanan ignore Douglas's importance to the party's operations and ideology, but he accepted the proslavery Lecompton Constitution from Kansas when it violated popular sovereignty as Douglas defined it. Then Buchanan deprived Douglas of the party's financial support and patronage, but overcoming that obstacle and as worthy an opponent as Lincoln to win reelection restored any political credibility that Douglas might have lost.

But only to a degree. In essence, Douglas represented the Democratic version of Seward or Chase. Like Chase, he could be too ambitious for his own good, not just when he ran for president before but in controlling his party in Illinois and in the Senate—thus did Greeley's *Tribune* say that "probably no other candidate for a presidential nomination ever played his hand so openly and boldly." Like Seward, he could be accused of adjusting his views to the moment. Douglas claimed to be a democrat—and Democrat—in every sense and opened himself to Lincoln's telling accusation that his claim of deferring to the people freed him from taking a position on anything, especially a moral issue such as slavery.[30]

Unfortunately for him, Douglas had tilted too far toward what would be described today as his party's left to unring the bells that went off among southern and northern proslavery Democrats— the right—at the mention of his name. For them, popular sovereignty could be neither popular nor sovereign. As convinced of a northern conspiracy against them as Republicans who believed in a slave power conspiracy between southerners and their northern allies, southern "fire-eaters" demanded the right to take their slaves anywhere without government interference. They and sympathetic Democrats saw the *Dred Scott* decision as the final word, making popular sovereignty unconstitutional on its face. When Douglas declared for his "gur-reat per-inciple" over a Supreme Court decision, he made himself anathema even to those in the Upper South and border states who preferred to douse the fire-eaters. Regardless, Douglas retained strong support among northern Democrats and unionist allies in the South and thus his status as the most serious contender for the nomination.

Besides, who else loomed as a possibility? Buchanan had made clear his plans to retire after one term, and few seemed to want him to change his mind. His vice president, John Breckinridge, could count on radical southerners and might appeal to border state voters as a Kentuckian. Secretary of the Treasury Howell Cobb wanted to be president, but his moderate background made him too soft for the fire-eaters and their allies. Cobb had worked with longtime Georgia Whigs Robert Toombs and Alexander Stephens to break the hold of older politicians on offices and patronage, but they had long since split. Cobb stuck to the Buchanan wing of the party, and the others backed Douglas out of personal loyalty and appreciation for the Compromise of 1850 and the Kansas-Nebraska Act. Some Georgians preferred Stephens, but he preferred Douglas and truly believed that if only the North would leave the South alone and Congress would leave slavery alone, everything would be all right—as great a misreading of matters as that of northerners who saw southerners as crying wolf. Nor, with fire-eaters insisting on power, would a ticket from both sides of the issue promote party unity. As a Democratic editor coarsely observed to a party leader who hoped to block Douglas's nomination, "I cannot see that it would tend to the triumph of social virtue were we to run a ticket with a very debauched whore on one end and a pure virgin on the other with a determination to be ruled by the one who got the most votes."[31]

Democrats appear not to have pondered one reason to turn aside Douglas: the dangers of a rematch. When Lincoln challenged him in 1858, Douglas understood that "I shall have my hands full. . . . He is as honest as he is shrewd; and if I beat him my victory will be hardly won." He later said that no senator ever gave him so much trouble in a debate as Lincoln did. Granted, they would hold no debates in 1860, but the closeness of the 1858 race and Lincoln's near victory served as a warning to both parties. Tackling the same tough opponent again, this time on a national scale, could pose problems for Douglas and the Democrats, while Republicans could view Lincoln's experience in campaigning against Douglas as yet another advantage. At the same time, either party could look at Lincoln's loss to Douglas in 1858—and Lincoln's subsequent rise often obscures that loss—as making him damaged goods, an unwise choice for the nomination.[32]

The Constitution, the Union, and the Impending Election

While Douglas drove toward the nomination and his foes flailed for an alternative, another party emerged from the ether—or, more accurately, from the remnants of the Whig and Know-Nothing Parties. Conservative northern Whigs and a substantial number of their southern counterparts had backed Fillmore on the American platform in 1856, often not out of nativism so much as a refusal to turn to a Democrat or an antislavery candidate. As the 1860 election approached, they remained hostile to both major parties, which they accused of diverging too much from the Constitution and a commitment to the Union. Thus, late in 1859, Senator John Crittenden of Kentucky convened about fifty border state and conservative members of Congress to form the Constitutional Union Party.

While Crittenden had no presidential ambitions, his involvement mattered symbolically. If anyone could claim Henry Clay's mantle of moderation and compromise, Crittenden could, to the degree that his letter supporting Douglas over Lincoln in the 1858 election bothered the Republican and aided the Democrat. Longtime Ohio politician John Allen believed that "many moderate Republicans and some democrats too look to a new party as a possible and not improbable harbor of refuge for them." The elder Francis Preston Blair wrote to Crittenden, an old friend from Kentucky despite their political differences, in hopes of enticing him to the Republican Party. Blair even suggested that he might become their presidential candidate as a means of reassuring the South. But Crittenden had no interest in a nomination from a party he agreed with, much less from one he disagreed with.[33]

If not to Crittenden, to whom would Constitutional Unionists turn? The "Houston mania," so called by New York conservative Washington Hunt, enveloped some of them. As a candidate, Sam Houston appealed to old Jacksonians with his military heroism in winning Texas independence, experience in national affairs, and staunch unionism as one of only two southern senators to back the Compromise of 1850. Popular enough in Tennessee and Texas to become the only man ever elected governor of two different states, Houston also struck those backing him as potentially dangerous— quick on the trigger in every sense—with fewer ties to the old Whigs who made up most of the party. As their convention approached in May 1860, other Constitutional Unionists looked to John Bell, the former senator from Tennessee whom *Harper's* accidentally converted into a Republican. After splitting with Jackson over his veto of the Second Bank of the United States, he remained a loyal Whig and had been the other southerner to vote with Houston in 1850.[34]

Thus, by the spring of 1860, politicians radical and conservative, North and South, had been maneuvering publicly or privately for the presidency. That so few outside of Illinois seemed aware that Lincoln was among them was a tribute to how carefully he staked his claim and lined up support. What John Randolph of Roanoke had said of Martin Van Buren was worth bearing in mind about Lincoln: he rowed to his object with muffled oars. Whether Lincoln would have appreciated the comparison is debatable: as a Whig and Republican, he fought Van Buren politically and had none of Randolph's states' rights mentality. From his quiet position as the first choice of few, as one of several on Seward's periphery as a Republican candidate in 1860, Lincoln was poised and positioned perfectly for the nomination—if the next steps in the process went his way.[35]

EVERYBODY'S SECOND CHOICE

Abraham Lincoln would spend an ordinary Friday at his law office or possibly at court. On May 18, 1860, he visited another attorney, then played handball, then walked the block back to the offices of Lincoln and Herndon and entertained two younger lawyers with stories before going to the telegraph office. Those around him thought Lincoln seemed jittery. He had a right to be. In Chicago, his party's national convention was choosing a presidential nominee. By that night, Lincoln would be not just a leading Illinois lawyer and politician but the country's most important Republican. He would owe that new status to the failings of his opponents, the devotion of his friends, and, above all, his political cunning.

"Give No Offence to Others"

In the spring of 1860, back from touring the Northeast, Lincoln continued to plot political strategy. Corresponding with Ohio editor and political boss Samuel Galloway, Lincoln tried to balance his ambitions with those of Salmon Chase, for whom Galloway had little use. Lincoln wrote, "I especially wish to do no ungenerous thing towards Governor Chase, because he gave us his sympathy in 1858, when scarcely any other distinguished man did." But Lincoln explained his chances to Galloway with clearer vision than Chase displayed, and not just because Chase was near-sighted. "My name is new in the field; and I suppose I am not the *first* choice of a very great many. Our policy, then, is to give no offence to others—leave them in a mood to come to us, if they shall be compelled to give up their first love," he wrote. He grasped that this approach promoted party unity: "This, too, is dealing justly with all, and leaving us in a mood to support heartily whoever shall be nominated." To a Connecticut editor hoping to correspond with Lincoln's "confidential friends," he suggested David Davis in Illinois, Galloway and fellow Ohioan Robert Schenck, and allies in Indiana and Iowa.[1]

Lincoln also mapped tactics to win the nomination, including pacifying feuding politicians and factions in Illinois. In Chicago on legal business, he apparently met with Norman Judd, who had aided Lincoln in his role as state chairman. Not only did Judd keep talking with his friends at the *Chicago Press and Tribune*, which continued to promote Lincoln. He also wrote to his friend Senator Lyman Trumbull about the importance of keeping William Henry Seward from building momentum and of uniting the Illinois delegation behind Lincoln as a means of heading off Edward Bates. Lincoln dealt with the continued intraparty battles—Judd on one side, Davis and Long John Wentworth on the other. He also talked with William Herndon and induced his law partner, a vociferous abolitionist, to stop his criticism of Judd.

Davis was normally a realist and a shrewd judge of men, but because Wentworth shared his distaste for Judd, he became carried away with his admiration for Long John. When Davis echoed Wentworth's criticism of Judd, Lincoln dealt with the problem partly by not dealing with it and by waiting for Davis to come around. In April, Davis told Lincoln, "I am more and more convinced of the wonderful power of John Wentworth," before lamenting his fight with Judd. But then Davis abandoned all logic. He reported the Chicago mayor's conviction that the *Press and Tribune*, one of the newspapers competing with his own, supported Seward and declared his agreement with Wentworth's interpretation. For the normally politic Davis, this was strange: the *Press and Tribune* had made clear its support for Lincoln, and, as a onetime Whig, Davis based his distrust for the Chicago paper on its origins in the Democratic party—to which Wentworth belonged before becoming a Republican. Then Davis explained to Lincoln, "Wentworth is for you decidedly and emphatically. He is for Seward in his paper for purposes that are satisfactory to me. The

Germans in Chicago love Gov. Seward. Judd is against Seward. Wentworth wants to beat Judd and must do it through the Dutch." Eventually Davis began to see friends like Wentworth and enemies like former Democrats Judd and Senator Trumbull differently, saying of "Long John" to Lincoln that "I think him insane almost on the subject of Judd" and "I don't think Trumbull is playing you false."[2]

How strongly Trumbull was on Lincoln's side mattered less than how wisely Lincoln used him, especially with the senator contemplating reelection in the next legislative session. Late in April, Trumbull wrote from Washington "candidly and frankly my impressions in regard to the Presidency, for such I know is the way you would desire me to speak, and I shall hope in return to be put fully in possession of your views." Trumbull concluded that in a race between Lincoln and Seward, the latter would win, partly because the "House Divided" speech struck a radical chord similar to Seward's "Irrepressible Conflict" and "Higher Law" speeches. Even if Lincoln had couched his argument, Trumbull wrote, "it matters not whether there is any foundation for this or not—I am not arguing the matter, but simply stating what others say." Trumbull's antenna proved more helpful when he reported on whether Republicans back east thought Seward could be elected. "The impression here is among all except his own friends that he cannot," that he lacked strength in Connecticut, Rhode Island, New Jersey, Indiana, and "Pennsylvania except Cameron," meaning the Keystone State's political boss favored Seward, but few others there did. But could Seward's nomination be blocked, and how? Trumbull leaned toward Supreme Court justice John McLean due to his support in Ohio and Pennsylvania. Yet he took great pains to reassure Lincoln, amid rumblings that McLean's nomination might lead to Trumbull's selection for vice president. "I do not wish you to understand that McLean would be my preference. . . . I wish to be distinctly understood as first and foremost for you," Trumbull wrote. "I want our state to send delegates not only instructed for you, but your friends who will stand by and nominate you if possible, never faltering unless you yourself shall so advise." Granting that Trumbull overrated McLean's chances, he also reinforced what Lincoln's strategy would have to be: finding a way around Seward.[3]

Early in April, Lincoln also made two speeches, confining himself to Illinois after his triumphant recent tour of New York and New England. At Waukegan, he rolled into a denunciation of slavery, but a fire broke out nearby, ending his speech and destroying several buildings. At Bloomington, he reverted to an earlier topic: the Mormon practice of polygamy or plural marriage. His party's platform in 1856 had declared it "both the right and the imperative duty of Congress to prohibit in the territories those twin relics of barbarism—Polygamy, and Slavery." Lincoln saw another contradiction to hammer in Stephen Douglas's popular sovereignty. A Douglas supporter in the House, John McClernand, had introduced a bill to divide Utah Territory, eliminating Mormon control. Douglas and his allies thought Congress should act against a territory's policies on marriage, whatever the view of the citizens living in it, Lincoln said. But leaving slavery alone, he argued, demonstrated the moral quagmire created by popular sovereignty.[4]

As he cautiously promoted himself, Lincoln subtly skewered his opponents. When a Cincinnati lawyer suggested that Lincoln could win more votes than Seward, Lincoln started with self-deprecation: "Remembering that when not a very great man begins to be mentioned for a very great position, his head is very likely to be a little turned . . ." Then he assessed his competitors. Seward struck him as "the very best candidate we could have for the North of Illinois and the very *worst* for the South of it," fitting the analysis popular among Seward's critics: he would do well among radicals and would cost Republicans in more conservative areas. Chase was "neither better nor worse . . . except that he is a newer man. They are regarded as being almost the same, seniority giving Seward the inside track." Bates was Seward's mirror image, "the best man for the south of our State, and the worst for the North of it." Deferring to conservatives, Lincoln repeated what he told Trumbull: if McLean "was fifteen, or even ten years younger, I think he would be stronger than either"—perhaps with the hope that others would agree, splitting Ohio's delegation. He also told Trumbull that much depended on the Democrats: if they chose Douglas, "neither Seward nor Bates can carry Illinois."[5]

Amid speaking, writing, and planning, Lincoln had another factor to consider: his wife, Mary. What role she played in his quest for the presidency, as in most of his political life, can only be conjectured. Clearly, while Lincoln was ambitious, she was ambitious for him. Their shared interest in politics had been one of their mutual attractions before their marriage, and they continued to share that interest as husband and wife. But in his relationship with Mary on political matters, Lincoln revealed the same shrewdness he did in his dealings with others. The 1855 Senate defeat had made her an enemy of Trumbull and Judd, but that did nothing to deter Lincoln from working with them, especially in 1860. As with his wife, so with his friends: Lincoln used what helped him and ignored what might hinder him.

By early May, Lincoln had sifted enough intelligence and received enough encouragement to venture a prediction, and it fit with his strategy. He told an Ohio supporter that he expected only the Illinois delegation to back him unanimously. "A few individuals in other delegations would like to go for me at the start, but may be restrained by their colleagues," he said. "[M]en who ought to know" believed that "the whole of Indiana might not be difficult to get," while from Ohio, "I have not heard that any one makes any positive objection to me. It is just so everywhere so far as I can perceive."[6]

The Birth of a Rail-Splitter

On May 9, 1860, about six hundred Illinois Republicans gathered in Decatur in a tent they called the "Wigwam." At a low point in the Judd-Wentworth feud, Lincoln had told Judd that "your assailants are most bitter against me; and they will, for revenge upon me, lay to the Bates egg in the south and to the Seward egg in the north." Beyond this homely metaphor, Lincoln took the occasion of his fifty-first birthday to ask Judd for a gift: "Can you not help me a little in this matter . . . ? It will not hurt much for me to not be nominated on the national ticket; but I am where it would hurt some for me to not get the Illinois delegates." Already having delivered the national convention to Chicago and apparently having brought the *Chicago Press and Tribune* to Lincoln's side, Judd would help Lincoln much more.[7]

Lincoln's arrival at the convention demonstrated the depth—more accurately, the height—of his popularity. Several weeks before, Governor William Bissell of Illinois wrote to Chase, "You have not a few friends in this state, among whom I count myself, who would be very glad to have you nominated at Chicago as our Presidential candidate; but our folks have recently taken a notion to talk up Lincoln for that place. Of course, while that is so, it would be ungracious and impolitic to start anybody as his seeming rival." By May, it was no longer "ungracious and impolitic" to back another candidate in Illinois; it was impossible. When they learned of Lincoln's presence, the delegates at the convention cheered lustily, picked him up, and carried him to the platform. According to one of them, "Lincoln was a mighty long man, but they carried him down over their heads right over everybody in the crowd. I have heard of that sort of thing, but never before nor since have I seen a long fellow like Lincoln passed hand over hand over a solid mass of people."[8]

Once Lincoln arrived on stage, Richard J. Oglesby spoke. A Decatur Republican, later a Union general, governor, and U.S. senator, he announced that an "old Democrat" from the region wanted to make a presentation. The delegates shouted, "Receive it! Receive it!" In came Isaac Jennings, joining John Hanks, a cousin of Lincoln's mother, Nancy. They toted two fence rails and a banner—"ABRAHAM LINCOLN THE RAIL CANDIDATE" —with an explanation that Lincoln had split the rails in 1830 and crediting Thomas Lincoln as a local pioneer. Called on to speak, Lincoln admitted that he could not prove that he split those two rails, but he did not correct the error in calling his father a pioneer, since Thomas Lincoln had quickly moved out of the area. But Lincoln confessed that he had split many rails and "mauled many and many better ones" since growing up.[9]

With the demonstrations and cheering over, the delegates tended to business. First, they debated the nominee for governor, with Lincoln wisely staying quiet. Judd led on the first ballot, followed by Leonard Swett, a Bloomington attorney and Lincoln's old friend and Whig ally, and Richard Yates, a former Whig congressman. But the divisions that cost Lincoln a Senate seat in 1855 bubbled back to the surface. Ex-Whigs sought to block Judd, and Wentworth and his allies made the mix especially combustible. Swett's backers switched to Yates, who won the nomination. Disappointed, Judd rose to the occasion with a speech calling so eloquently for unity that even many of his foes praised him and supported his reelection as state chair. And the delegates united behind Lincoln. They passed a resolution recognizing him as "the choice of the Republican party of Illinois for the Presidency, and the delegates from this State are instructed to use all honorable means to secure his nomination by the Chicago Convention, and to vote as a unit for him." When a Seward supporter tried to speak in opposition, the chair and the delegates quickly quashed him.[10]

The convention also deferred to Lincoln, letting him pick four of the twenty-two national convention delegates. He sat down in a grove near the Wigwam with Judd, Swett, Davis, and several other Republicans to choose the slate. Again, Lincoln proved his shrewdness. He chose Gustave Koerner, the leading member of the party's German group in Illinois, to represent him to a constituency that appreciated Seward's battles with nativists and opposed Bates for joining with them. He also tapped Judd, who should have gone anyway, both as state chairman and for having done so much to deliver the national convention to Chicago. That decision bothered Davis and his choice for an at-large delegate, Wentworth, who could hardly be on the slate with Judd. Lincoln also knew Judd would work tirelessly for him. With Wentworth, that would be less certain.

Lincoln's other choices appealed to ex-Whigs. Alleviating Davis's displeasure that Judd would be a delegate and Wentworth would not, Lincoln chose the judge. Davis figured to be in Chicago, but only as an ally without portfolio. Lincoln's decision made clear that Davis would be in the thick of things. His other choice, Orville Browning, remained so Whiggish that he told Lincoln that he preferred Bates—and Lincoln dealt with his friend so carefully and subtly that Browning thought he agreed. But after twenty years of friendship, Lincoln expected loyalty to trump politics. When others objected to including Browning, Lincoln reportedly replied that he "will do more harm on the outside than he could on the inside" and felt "satisfied that Bates has no show. When Orville sees this he'll undoubtedly come over to me, and do us some good with the Bates men." Events proved him right.[11]

The state convention proved especially important for Lincoln for several reasons. Since presidential candidates were supposed to stay above the fray, or at least seem to do so, it marked the last time he could work transparently on his own behalf, and he took advantage of the opportunity. His state's delegates gave him what he wanted and needed: their unanimous support. New York would do the same for Seward, but Lincoln's other major competitors lacked their good fortune: Ohio remained divided over Chase, and whatever Missouri's delegates did for Bates at the convention, their support would mean less than the united front from Illinois. Lincoln had put the right people in place to help him without giving too much offense to those he had bypassed.

More important for Lincoln's future, the convention also gave him an image for the public to embrace. Democrats had benefited for three decades by promoting Andrew Jackson as Old Hickory and by linking him to those who sought to emulate him, from using Martin Van Buren's New York hometown for the unexciting "Old Kinderhook" to James Polk's appropriate "Young Hickory" and Franklin Pierce's silly "Young Hickory from the Granite Hills." By 1840, Whigs learned and ran William Henry Harrison's "Log Cabin and Hard Cider" campaign, then "Old Rough and Ready" Zachary Taylor in 1848. Lincoln had taken little or no political advantage of his hardscrabble beginnings, which he had spent nearly three decades trying to escape. He had risen in society as a successful attorney and married into a leading Kentucky family; he had a wife who undertook a lifelong effort to civilize him as part of a political party associated with the elite, at times to his—and the elite's—detriment. Thanks to an Illinois politician and a cousin—from the side of his family that he suspected of holding a higher social rank than the Lincolns—he had suddenly become and could help fashion an image of himself as "The Rail-Splitter." Now he was the kind of candidate who could appeal to the free-labor "mudsills," a term that South Carolina's James Henry Hammond used in the Senate to deride common laborers in the North. But those laborers could vote.

"Lincoln Ain't Here"

A week after the Illinois convention, Republicans came to another Wigwam. This one, a 180-by-100-foot, two-story structure built at the intersection of Lake Street and Market Street in Chicago at a cost of five thousand dollars to house the national convention, could hold ten thousand delegates from northern, border, and a couple of Upper South slave states, journalists, hangers-on, and spectators. Not the candidates themselves: that would have been unseemly. So, Seward waited in Auburn, Chase in Columbus, Bates outside St. Louis, and Lincoln in Springfield. With his friends telling him to stay home, Lincoln mused, "I am a little too much a candidate to stay home and not quite enough a candidate to go." But his presence loomed in the Wigwam and the hotels where delegates brokered their party's fate.[12]

Lincoln continued to aid his cause. He paid the way for Mark Delahay, an Illinois friend who moved to Kansas, to go to the Chicago convention and suggested that he lobby other western delegates from Iowa and Minnesota while being "careful to give no offence, and keep cool under all circumstances." He warned Illinois delegates and managers against discussing the tariff, which could be controversial, but provided a written assurance that he wanted kept confidential if possible. "In the days of Henry Clay I was a Henry Clay-tariff-man; and my views have undergone no material change upon that subject," he said. As the convention began, he wrote a note to Davis, his chief manager: "I agree with Seward in his 'Irrepressible Conflict,' but I do not endorse his 'Higher Law' doctrine. *Make no contracts that bind me*," positioning himself as moderate and instructing his managers. And whether or not Lincoln had anything to do with it, William Herndon stayed in Springfield, tending to the legal business that was the farthest thing from his law partner's mind, and not in Chicago making radical pronouncements that might derail Lincoln's candidacy or haunt him later.[13]

If Lincoln as president brought together a ministry of all the talents from across his party, a similar constellation of Illinois political talent represented him at the convention and reflected his wishes. Davis benefited from two decades as an Illinois judge and a backroom operator in Whig and Republican councils. Swett, his closest ally, another Whig lawyer experienced at campaigning and king-making, recalled Davis telling the Illinoisans, "If you will put yourself at my disposal day and night, I believe Lincoln can be nominated." One of his fellow operatives said he "never saw him work so hard and so quick in his life." According to Swett, "No one ever thought of questioning Davis' right to send men hither and thither, nor to question his judgment." After the convention, Lyman Trumbull's brother-in-law told him that the Illinoisans "worked like Turks for Lincoln's nomination."[14]

Davis's judgment proved sound—and so did Lincoln's in giving him the human tools with which to operate. Swett had come to Illinois from Maine, so he worked on that delegation, which already showed signs of wanting anyone but Seward. Koerner dealt with German constituents, Judd with old Democrats. Longstanding Lincoln allies like state auditor Jesse Dubois and Springfield politician William Butler moved among delegations at Davis's command. Browning provided ballast in dealing with conservative Whigs, especially from Indiana. Nor did it hurt Lincoln's chances that *Press and Tribune* editors Joseph Medill and Charles Ray pounded delegates with editorials explaining Lincoln's potential as a nominee and the problems with all of the other possible choices. "He occupies the happy mean between that alleged radicalism which binds the older Anti-Slavery men to Mr. Seward, and that conservatism which dictates the support of Judge Bates," the Chicago daily announced the day before the convention began. "Without a stain of Know-Nothingism on his skirts, he is acceptable to the mass of the American party." Lincoln's history as a Whig also made him a safe choice for those hankering for Henry Clay's reincarnation or for tariffs and internal improvements.[15]

That editorial represented a shot across Seward's bow, and Thurlow Weed stood ready to volley back. The New York Republican boss and his allies arrived early, ready to use a heavy hand in offering money, alcohol, and patronage. Weed could count on support from New York and much of New England. But, adept at counting noses, Weed knew that several states planned to back favorite sons and was aware of the doubts about Seward's radicalism and probity. Weed read the omens incorrectly, telling Seward, "Lincoln's Friends started him only for the second place, for which I immediately accepted him," while Butler told Lincoln, "We have persistently refused to suffer your name used for Vice President on any ticket." Worse for Seward, just as New York Republicans often split between radicals and conservatives, or ex-Democrats and ex-Whigs, so did other states. The more they divided, the better Lincoln's chances. The nominee needed 233 votes or just over half of the delegates to win, and even with his juggernaut arriving from Albany and other points east, Seward seemed unlikely to carry the convention on the first ballot. Thus, from the beginning, Lincoln had a chance if the balloting went on long enough and Seward's support started to wane.[16]

Lincoln benefited from others determined to block the New Yorker. Denied a seat in the New York delegation, Horace Greeley wangled one from Oregon, giving him more than the usual journalistic access to the convention. He made the most of it, circulating among delegates while wearing a Seward badge (possibly pinned on him without his knowledge) and warning that Seward could not be elected. Meanwhile, Francis Preston Blair and his sons—Montgomery of Maryland and Frank Jr. of Missouri—used their contacts among old Democrats and in the border states to whip up anti-Seward sentiment. They still backed Bates but cared more about stopping Seward. Republicans aghast at Democratic corruption during the 1850s feared Weed's reputation and influence over Seward and the ease with which he offered to lubricate the party machinery with money. And other politicians had other ambitions: would-be senators and governors, especially in Pennsylvania and Indiana, knew that any vote-getting problems for the national Republican ticket in 1860 would percolate down to the local level, hurting their chances.

On Monday, May 14, two days before the convention opened, Lincoln's managers saw signs of trouble. Thirteen railroad cars with two thousand Seward delegates and supporters poured into Chicago, a sign of the formidable opposition Lincoln's men faced. As one of them wrote the day before, "Our delegation will stick to Lincoln as long as there is a chance to prevent Seward getting any votes from us at all." Nonetheless, the Illinois delegates also had a problem in their midst, or more accurately, on their periphery. Wentworth remained upset that Lincoln would acknowledge Judd's existence, much less favor him. Not only did he trumpet Seward's candidacy in editorials, but he also used his power as mayor to order a raid on local brothels, doing nothing to endear anyone from Illinois to some of the convention-goers. Lincoln used good judgment in keeping one potential loose cannon, Browning, close to him; whether he had been equally wise in keeping a looser cannon, Wentworth, far away remained to be seen.[17]

Other signs pointed in Lincoln's direction. Pennsylvania Republicans were as divided as ever and feuding with New Yorkers, making Weed's hopes of capturing that state and holding onto it for Seward less likely. More crucially, Lincoln's decision to include Koerner as a delegate paid off. Republicans also needed Indiana if they hoped to win the presidency, and Koerner spoke to its delegates, who included a number of German-Americans. He recalled saying "that if Bates was nominated, the German Republicans in the other States would never vote for him; I for one would not, and I would advise my countrymen to the same effect." His appeal helped capture that delegation, as did longtime Indiana politician Caleb Smith, more conservative on slavery than Lincoln but a fellow ex-Whig who had known Lincoln when they served in the House. Delahay wrote to Lincoln, "Indiana is all right." That moved Lincoln closer to what Davis deemed necessary: 100 delegates on the first ballot to establish him as Seward's strongest challenger. "Your friends are at work for you hard, and with great success. Your show on the first ballot will not be confined to Illinois, and after that it will be strongly developed," newspaperman Charles Ray apprised Lincoln. Another ally, Nathan Knapp, wrote, "We have got Seward in the attitude of the representative Republican of the East—you of the West." Left unsaid—Lincoln knew it anyway—was the value of positioning him that way: the West was crucial to Republican chances that fall.[18]

The next day, May 15, brought more of the same. A Minnesota delegate noted that Weed, ever attentive to detail, "told me he had been looking anxiously for me, to keep our men right." Other Illinois delegates arrived that morning and spread the message: Seward was too radical to win and Lincoln could appeal to a broader spectrum of voters. Davis revisited the Maine and Massachusetts delegations, this time with Browning—as Lincoln predicted, a staunch ally. A Democrat until the birth of the Republicans, John Palmer joined Davis to address the New Jersey delegates, who wanted a Seward-Lincoln ticket. Palmer's background enhanced his credibility when he explained that old Illinois Democrats would never vote Republican if the ticket consisted of two ex-Whigs. Butler notified Lincoln that "Pennsylvania will never go for Seward," whose campaign had offered to fund the fall campaign for Illinois Republicans if Lincoln would accept the vice presidential nomination. Davis and Jesse Dubois reported to Lincoln in a telegram: "We are quiet but moving heaven & Earth nothing will beat us but old fogy politicians the heart of the delegates are with us." Dubois added, "Prospects very good we are doing everything Illinois men acting nobly Browning doing his duty."[19]

Although other Illinois Republicans did their duty, Judd outdid them all, with the exception of Davis as commander of Lincoln's troops, with two major steps that aided Lincoln's cause immeasurably. First, Judd delivered on one of his arguments for holding the convention in Chicago by using his connections to cut railroad fares. While that could benefit anyone who came to the convention, it enabled large numbers of Illinoisans to fill the galleries, and they cheered almost constantly for Lincoln. Also, Judd obtained the authority to determine where delegations would sit in the convention hall—a logical job for the local chair. He later said, "I put New York about the centre on the right hand side, and grouped New England, Wisconsin, Minnesota, and all the strong Seward States immediately around her." On the other side, he grouped Illinois and Indiana, with Pennsylvania "within a handshaking distance." Thus, he reasoned, "when the active excitement and canvassing in the Convention came on, the Seward men couldn't get over among the doubtful delegations at all to log-roll with them, being absolutely hemmed in by their own followers who were not likely to be swerved from their set preference for Seward." But the most important delegations, from states that Republicans lost in 1856 and needed to win in 1860, would be near one another—and Weed and his group would have a hard time reaching them on the convention floor.[20]

The first day of the convention, May 16, marked Seward's birth-day, and it would not prove an altogether happy one for him. Murat Halstead told *Cincinnati Commercial* readers, "The current of the uni-versal twaddle this morning is that 'Old Abe' will be the nominee," although he gave no reason why; perhaps holding the convention in Chicago and providing easy access to Illinoisans created the effect for which Lincoln and his supporters hoped. That Wednesday and Thursday, thousands jammed the Wigwam as the convention came to order, listened to welcoming speeches, and approved a platform. It immediately became clear that the Republicans hoped to avoid controversy and largely did so. The platform committee, comprised mostly of moderate westerners, softened the 1856 platform's attack on slavery and condemned John Brown's raid. Old abolitionist Joshua Giddings requested a provision endorsing the statement in the Dec-laration of Independence that all men are created equal. But the committee hoped to avoid amendments and blocked him, prompt-ing Giddings to walk out of the convention hall. Another delegate delivered a speech on Giddings's behalf, the convention amended the platform, and Giddings returned to his seat.[21]

The procedural votes favored Seward, instilling confidence in Weed and his allies and revealing the alternating waves of euphoria and depression afflicting those at the convention. Distressed, Greeley reported to the *New York Tribune*, "My conclusion, from all that I can gather to-night, is that the opposition to . . . Seward cannot concentrate on any candidate, and that he will be nominated." Hal-stead agreed that "the universal impression was that Seward's success was certain." Delahay lamented to Lincoln, "Your men are I regret to say too honest to advance your prospects as easily as I would like to see; *Davis* is a good judge doubtless and Duboise [*sic*] and Butler are honest and faithful but they are unacquainted with New York Polaticians [*sic*]. I live among them and have suffered at their hands." But the Illinoisans remained optimistic. Judd telegraphed, "Don't be frightened Keep cool things is working," and Davis added, "Am very hopeful don't be excited nearly dead with fatigue."[22]

Davis had reason to be hopeful. Aware that momentum seemed to have shifted toward Seward and of the need to regain it, Davis belied Delahay's perception of him. The judge realized that if Lincoln survived the first ballot, he would have to make an impression on the second ballot, meaning the need for another large state delegation to switch to him. Pennsylvania remained up for grabs, and Davis decided to snatch it. Apparently bringing Swett and Ray, he cloistered himself with a Pennsylvania group headed by Joseph Casey, a former Whig congressman. Casey knew Davis had come close to winning New Jersey's support for Lincoln, Pennsylvania was the only uncommitted swing state, and Lincoln and Davis needed Pennsylvania more than Pennsylvania needed them. That gave Casey a great bargaining chip on behalf of his friend Simon Cameron, and he used it: if Davis wanted Pennsylvania's delegation, he had to take Cameron as a member of Lincoln's cabinet, ideally as secretary of the treasury.[23]

What happened—or not—became part of Lincoln lore. In a "Profoundly Private" letter, Ray told Lincoln just before the convention that "you need a few trusty friends here to say words for you that may be necessary to be said. . . . A pledge or two may be necessary when the pinch comes. Don't be too sanguine." Regardless of how Lincoln felt, Davis saw the pinch had come. Supposedly reminded that Lincoln said, "Make no contracts that will bind me," Davis replied, "Lincoln ain't here." Casey emerged from the meeting sure that Cameron would be in the cabinet, but did Davis make such a promise? Davis said he told Casey that his state probably would have a seat at Lincoln's table, which hardly bound him: as a swing state, Pennsylvania could expect no less. After all, Franklin Pierce named a Pennsylvanian to the key patronage job of postmaster general, and in 1856, Democrats nominated a Pennsylvanian, Buchanan. But who from that state would serve in Lincoln's cabinet? Casey thought Davis had been specific, but Davis claimed only to have promised to *suggest* Cameron. Ray apparently told fellow editor Medill that the promise had been made; Alexander McClure of Pennsylvania, another participant, recalled that only after the delegates shifted to Lincoln did Davis assure them that Cameron would have a cabinet post. What mattered most was that Davis left the meeting and told the *Press and Tribune*, "Damned if we haven't got them." How, a reporter asked. Davis replied, "By paying their price."[24]

How much of a price Davis—and thus Lincoln—paid remains open to question. Historian David Potter refers to "the overall dualism in the folklore which has presented the alternative images of a godlike man of sorrows," Lincoln, whose martyrdom was unimaginable in 1860, "and an earthy frontier trickster," Davis. Many historians have argued that the "frontier trickster" promised the cabinet posts. That is debatable—and ironic, given the many tales of Lincoln's frontier cleverness—but depicting Davis in that way meant leaguing him with Lincoln, whose westernness and shrewdness long have played a part in the fact and fiction written about him, while also distinguishing the judge from "Honest Abe."[25]

But any promises ultimately may have done nothing to win over delegates and hardly would have been unusual. Even if Davis went further than his candidate preferred, Lincoln never disavowed him. Given Lincoln's talent for looking at issues from the perspective opposite of his own and for political maneuvering, Davis probably did nothing that Lincoln would not have done if their roles had been reversed. And Davis said later, "Mr. Lincoln is committed to no one on earth in relation to office—He promised nothing to gain his nomination, and has promised nothing," although that did not mean that Davis promised nothing. Years later, when asked, "You must have prevaricated somewhat?" Davis replied, "PREVARICATED? . . . We lied, lied like hell."[26]

Another factor, doubtless more important than anything Davis promised, was the nature of Pennsylvania politics. As an ex-Whig, Seward boasted the right economic credentials on the protective tariff, a favorite issue in the Keystone State. In March 1859, after speaking with Cameron, he told Weed, "He was for me, and Pennsylvania would be." As the convention neared, though, Cameron refused to answer Weed's letters or meet with him. Given Seward's baggage—especially his radicalism on slavery, since any state party led by Cameron could hardly condemn Seward as corrupt—Pennsylvania had yet to guarantee him its votes. Also, Know-Nothings had been strong there, and Seward's anti-nativist principles came back to haunt him. Indeed, the only thing on which Pennsylvania's delegates may have been able to agree was to oppose Seward. But whom to support? Although he worked with Know-Nothings in Ohio, albeit to promote antislavery interests, Chase subscribed to the old Democratic orthodoxy against a protective tariff, and Bates was barely a Republican, if at all. Whatever deals Davis made, Casey had heard from David Wilmot, of Proviso fame, that Lincoln was worthy of consideration. Lincoln had established himself as a candidate and made clear that his Whiggish economic views accompanied him into the Republican Party.[27]

The divisions between ex-Democrats and ex-Whigs within the Republican Party also may have affected Pennsylvania. John Shaffer, an Illinoisan who preferred Cameron but was pledged to Lincoln, told Swett that Seward's and Cameron's supporters at the convention would switch to Ohioan Ben Wade. Shaffer explained that Lincoln's support from Judd and the *Press and Tribune* made Cameron's backers suspicious of their fate when the time would come for Lincoln to dole out patronage. "I got all my Illinois friends of the Cameron & Seward element together. My assurance to them was this—That I knew you to be a fair minded man & if elected you would treat all fairly," Swett informed Lincoln. "After consulting Davis, I gave them the most solemn assurances I am capable of giving, that they should not only not be proscribed but that by-gones should be by-gones & they should be placed upon the same footing as if originally they had been your friends." Thus, the pledge of equitable treatment, and not necessarily that Cameron would enter the cabinet, may have helped win over his delegates.[28]

Another version of events suggested that Davis had no need to make promises and played a smaller role than believed. Thomas Dudley, a New Jersey delegate who later became an American consul in Europe, later claimed that delegates from his state, Illinois, Indiana, and Pennsylvania held a meeting before the voting. There, Governor John Andrew of Massachusetts and the New England delegation laid out for them how Seward's nomination would cost Republicans their chances for the presidency. Accordingly, after considerable discussion, the state delegations agreed: once the complimentary balloting ended on the first round, New Jersey would drop its favorite son, William Dayton, if Pennsylvania would abandon Cameron, and then they would back Lincoln. The account seems unlikely—events on the convention floor poke holes in Dudley's version—but the idea of such a meeting and plan is plausible.[29]

Whatever promises had been made, the next day, May 18, the balloting began. One of Lincoln's supporters telegraphed Elihu Washburne, a congressman from Illinois, "Lincoln will be nominated. I think he is the second choice of everybody." First, though, came some anxious moments: an Indiana delegate suggested a first ballot favorite son vote for Caleb Smith, who stayed loyal to Lincoln and rejected the proposal, and Seward's nomination caused a boisterous display. But when Judd stood and declared, "I desire on behalf of the delegation from Illinois, to put in nomination as a candidate for President of the United States, Abraham Lincoln of Illinois," the roar was equally deafening, if not more so, thanks partly to some leather-lunged spectators whom Lincoln's supporters apparently compensated for their efforts. When Indiana's Smith seconded Judd, it should have been a sign of something brewing with that key state. After other nominations, the delegations started voting, with Seward weaker than expected in New England and Lincoln gaining help from Virginia. By the end of the first ballot, Seward had 173½ votes, 60 shy of the nomination. Lincoln's team had done its work well: he had 102 votes, placing him second with slightly more delegates than Davis hoped for, and Seward lacked the votes to win. The promises Davis and his foot soldiers extracted from several delegations to make Lincoln their second choice figured to bear fruit. At the telegraph office just north of the capitol building in Springfield, Lincoln read the results. "From the manner in which Mr. Lincoln received this dispatch, it was my impression that it was as favorable as he expected," one observer noted.[30]

The second ballot proved even more favorable. The New Hampshire delegation coalesced around Lincoln. After a first ballot bouquet to a favorite son, elderly Vermont senator Jacob Collamer delivered what Murat Halstead called "a blighting blow upon the Seward interests" by switching its 10 votes to Lincoln, as its delegates promised. Then, after meeting privately, 44 of the 46 Pennsylvanians committed to Cameron switched to Lincoln. As the second ballot ended, Seward had gained only 11 delegates while Lincoln jumped to 181. Halstead wrote, "It now dawned upon the multitude that the presumption entertained the night before, that the Seward men would have everything their own way, was a mistake." If momentum mattered, and it did, it had shifted to Lincoln. The New York delegates at Weed's command proved unable to move against it—literally. Judd's mapping of the convention floor had hemmed them in, keeping them away from the Ohio, New Jersey, and Missouri delegations, all up for grabs as the third ballot began.[31]

On the third ballot, the improbable became not just possible but reality. Four Massachusetts delegates shifted from Seward to Lincoln. New Jersey gave up on favorite son William Dayton, with most of its delegates going to Lincoln. When Ohio's turn came, the groundwork Lincoln laid and his supporters built on paid off as 15 delegates switched. Oregon, where Greeley sat, moved some of its votes from Bates to Lincoln. As the third ballot ended, Seward fell to 180 while Lincoln rose to 231½, one and a half votes shy of the nomination. The Wigwam, filled with noisy Lincoln supporters, fell silent.

Then David Cartter stood. Earlier that day, as chair of the Ohio delegation, he had nominated Chase for president. Cartter later claimed to have been promised a patronage job, and Medill allegedly told him that if Lincoln won Ohio's vote, "Chase can have anything he wants." Normally, Cartter stuttered, but no one had trouble understanding what he said and what it meant: "I rise (eh), Mr. Chairman (eh), to announce the change of four votes of Ohio from Mr. Chase to Mr. Lincoln." Halstead wrote, "There was a moment's silence. The nerves of the thousands, which through the hours of suspense had been subjected to terrible tension, relaxed, and as deep breaths of relief were taken, there was a noise in the wigwam like the rush of a great wind, in the van of a storm—and in another breath, the storm was there. There were thousands cheering with the energy of insanity."[32]

Abraham Lincoln would be the Republican nominee for president in 1860. Other delegations began switching their votes. Finally, William Evarts, a New York attorney and politician, future U.S. senator and secretary of state, and Seward ally who had placed his friend's name in nomination, stood before the convention. He admitted his disappointment but then proclaimed, "I move, Sir, as I do now that the nomination of Abraham Lincoln of Illinois as the Republican candidate for the suffrages of the whole country for the office of Chief Magistrate of the American Union be made unanimous." And it was.[33]

Two men wept. In the New York delegation, Thurlow Weed buried his face in his hands and sobbed, heartbroken that the prize for which he had worked for so long for Seward had slipped from their grasp. Back in Auburn, New York, townspeople put away the cannon they planned to fire in honor of their native son's nomination as president. As Halstead described Seward's supporters in Chicago, "They were mortified beyond all expression, and walked thoughtfully and silently away from the slaughterhouse, more ashamed than embittered." Meanwhile, overcome with joy and exhaustion, David Davis burst into tears. To Davis, "more than to any other man," Jesse Fell later said, belonged credit for shepherding Lincoln's campaign through the convention.[34]

Two men were thrilled, but only one showed it. Seated with Oregon's delegates, Horace Greeley reportedly beamed at avenging Weed's denial of support for his political ambitions. In Springfield, Lincoln moved from the telegraph office to the *Illinois State Journal* office to await the outcome. When several friends arrived from the telegraph office to tell him the news, one said that amid the handshakes, "a close observer could detect strong emotions within." Lincoln said, "Well, I guess I will go and tell my wife about it; she cares more about it than I do." That statement seems typically Lincolnian—amusing, ironic, unemotional—but it had a ring of truth: Lincoln had tried to avoid becoming too hopeful, and Mary long had been convinced that he was destined for high office. That night, a crowd surrounded the house at Eighth and Jackson until Lincoln came out to respond to its serenade by declaring that their support was more for the party and the cause than for him, and his house was too small to invite in everyone. Someone shouted, "We will give you a larger house on the fourth of next March."[35]

Reacting in Springfield

While the Senate race against Douglas had changed his life, what happened in Chicago on May 18, 1860, changed Lincoln's life even more. From his friends and allies came congratulations and advice. Davis wired, "Don't come here for God's sake," and added, "Write no letters and make no promises till you see me," perhaps so that Lincoln could find out what Davis had promised. Ray, Medill, and John L. Scripps of the *Press and Tribune* advised him not to "come here till after New York has gone home," suggesting a fear that Weed might be up to something. Nathan Knapp simply wrote, "We did it. Glory to God," and Fell, one of the first of Lincoln's friends to think seriously about his candidacy, added, "From my inmost heart I congratulate you." From Washington, Trumbull wrote that "our friends are greatly rejoiced. A large majority of the Republican members of Congress have all the time feared Mr. Seward's nomination, and it was a great relief when the news came. All was bustle in both Houses. . . . I look upon Illinois as now safe to the Republicans in all its departments, and upon your election as a fixed fact. Glory to God, the country is safe." Wentworth offered nothing congratulatory but provided the news that Hannibal Hamlin, a onetime Democrat from Maine, would be Lincoln's running mate. The second choice had been Cassius Clay, whose abolitionism would have done little to improve the party's support among border state voters, although Clay came from Kentucky.[36]

Lincoln's life as his party's nominee formally began with the delegation to notify him of his selection. The convention's presiding officer, George Ashmun of Massachusetts, telegraphed him on May 18 and led a group to Springfield the next day, with the Illinois Central Railroad, one of Lincoln's clients, paying the way. When the committee arrived at about 8:00 PM, Ashmun read the address, and Lincoln accepted, thanked him, and promised to write something later. When Ashmun made introductions, Lincoln asked one of the delegates, William Kelley of Pennsylvania, how tall he was. When he turned out to be an inch shorter than Lincoln's six-foot-four, Kelley replied, "Then Pennsylvania bows to Illinois. My dear man, for years my heart has been aching for a President that I could *look up to*, and I've found him at last in the land where we thought there were none but *little giants*." Noting Lincoln's "new but ill-fitting clothes, his long tawny neck emerging gauntly from his turn-down collar, his melancholy eyes sunken deep in his haggard face," Carl Schurz felt that "the hearty simplicity of Lincoln's nature shone out." Another said, "I was afraid I should meet a gigantic rail-splitter, with the manners of a flatboatman, and the ugliest face in creation; and he's a complete gentleman!" Within a couple of days came another in a long line of letters. "You can hardly imagine, and I am sure I can not describe my feelings when I saw by the papers this morning that you were a candidate for the Presidency," Joshua Speed wrote from Louisville. "Allow a warm personal friend, though as you are perhaps aware, a political opponent, to congratulate you. Should you be elected and I think you have a fair chance for it, I am satisfied that you will honestly administer the government—and make a lasting reputation for yourself."[37]

Speed had known Lincoln since his arrival in Springfield nearly a quarter of a century before and knew more of his hopes and ambitions than his other friends did. While Lincoln long had sought advancement and to make a difference, only since the Republican Party's creation had he moved to the political forefront in a way that suggested he had a future in public office. His defeat for the Senate in 1855 and the flurry for his vice presidential nomination at the 1856 convention had marked him as more than just one of the leading Whigs from the only truly Whig area in Illinois. The campaign against Stephen Douglas had catapulted Lincoln to prominence, and then he and his friends and allies took advantage of that fact to propel him to the presidential nomination. Some events were beyond their control: Seward's reputation, Greeley's anger, Chase's ego. But Lincoln brought to his quest for the presidency both character and talents not yet evident to the rest of the world: a moral commitment to stopping the spread of slavery, a sense of political realities, and the ability to negotiate between them with men of differing views and to link them through the brilliant use of language that could be beautiful, earthy, or both.

As critical as these talents were, Lincoln and the Illinois Republicans surrounding him, especially Davis and Judd, did something else: they made none of the mistakes their counterparts did. Lincoln and his advisers knew what to say, when and where to say it, whom to cultivate, and whom to ignore. They struck deals at the right time and place, avoided overconfidence or diffidence, and, for the most part, sublimated their egos in common cause. Now that Illinoisans had managed that, Republicans from across the country would have to do the same—and hope that events broke in their direction.[38]

FROM CANDIDATE TO LEADER

Nineteenth-century political conventions often chose a nominee's running mate for him or with his behind-the-scenes con-
nivance. Who would be the Republican vice presidential candidate
in 1860 was beyond the immediate interest of Abraham Lincoln or
his allies, who had had enough to do to win the nomination without
worrying about the rest of the ticket. When Lincoln learned that he
would run with Senator Hannibal Hamlin of Maine, he displayed
a desire for cooperation in taking the first step despite being above
Hamlin on the ticket. "It appears to me that you and I ought to be
acquainted, and accordingly I write this as a sort of introduction of
myself to you," he wrote. "I shall be pleased to receive a line from
you. The prospect of Republican success now appears very flatter-
ing, so far as I can perceive. Do you see anything to the contrary?"[1]

The letter foreshadowed and disguised Lincoln's role in the campaign. He could say little on his own behalf, since presidential candidates were supposed to be rarely seen and more rarely heard. His
desire to be kept up-to-date suggested a normal curiosity. In his
case, that curiosity meant transcending the roles played by Whig
and Republican nominees he had supported and Democrats he had
opposed. As Richard Carwardine observes in his political biography
of Lincoln, "An instinctive electoral strategist, as well as a salient
campaigner in every presidential contest since 1840, he had no inten-
tion of placing his future exclusively in the hands of others." He had
been the architect of the necessary steps to be nominated. During

the 1860 campaign, no one took more care to assure a Republican victory, or strategized more carefully about how to achieve it, than Abraham Lincoln.[2]

"You Mistake Us"

Just after the 1858 election, a year and a half before the conventions, Lincoln assessed Stephen Douglas's chances of winning the Democratic nomination. Aware that Douglas had broken with President James Buchanan and burned his bridges behind him as he did, and that southerners abhorred his refusal to accept the *Dred Scott* case as settling the question of slavery in the territories, Lincoln told Senator Lyman Trumbull of Illinois, "The majority of the democratic politicians of the nation mean to kill him; but I doubt whether they will adopt the aptest way to do it." As a veteran of politics and careful observer of Douglas, Lincoln reasoned, "Their true way is to present him with no new test, let him into the Charleston Convention, and then outvote him, and nominate another." That would defeat Douglas in a way that exemplified the democracy in which he claimed to believe. Lincoln noted, "In that case, he will have no pretext for bolting the nomination, and will be as powerless as they can wish." But he foresaw another possibility: "If they push a Slave code upon him, as a test, he will bolt at once, turn upon us, as in the case of Lecompton, and claim that all Northern men shall make common cause in electing him President as the best means of breaking down the Slave Power."[3]

During and after the Senate race in 1858, Lincoln sought to keep Republicans from allying with Douglas. The Little Giant did all he could to help achieve that goal. When a southern senator requested an investigation into John Brown's raid on Harpers Ferry in hopes of finding a Republican connection, Douglas endorsed it, describing Brown's "crimes" as "the natural, logical, inevitable result of the doctrines and teachings of the Republican party." As in the debates, he accused Republicans of promoting racial equality—not the kind of rhetoric associated with someone seeking any sort of political fusion—and said, "I do not admit the fact that there is a better Democrat on earth than I am, or a sounder one on the question of

State rights, and even on the slavery question." Yet he warned the Senate—and, in turn, other Democrats—that "I am not seeking a nomination. I am willing to take one provided I can assume it on principles that I believe to be sound; but in the event of your making a platform that I could not conscientiously execute in good faith if I were elected, I will not stand upon it and be a candidate."[4]

Obviously, though, Douglas wanted the nomination. He sought it as ardently as Lincoln did, but as the known front-runner instead of as a dark horse, he could not help but be transparent. Douglas devoted considerable time in late 1859 and early 1860 to cementing friendships, especially in the Old Northwest. He managed his state convention only slightly less than Lincoln's advisers did in Decatur. Like Lincoln, he faced intraparty divisions, but the Democratic split over slavery took a different turn: among northerners, how much they sympathized with southerners; among southerners, whether Douglas sympathized enough with them. Several states, especially in the South, proposed favorite sons but none to match Douglas's support, especially in the North. Still, he prepared carefully. Perhaps conscious of Norman Judd's coup in winning the convention for Lincoln's home turf in Chicago, Douglas and his top advisers pushed Illinoisans to make the long trip to Charleston, South Carolina, to fill the galleries and influence the delegates on the floor. Two days before the Democratic convention, Lincoln hedged his analysis, possibly because he understood Douglas's ability to cause a fight where none existed or to use trickery or demagoguery to come out ahead. "Opinions here, as to the prospect of Douglas being nominated, are quite conflicting," Lincoln said. "I think his nomination possible; but that the chances are against him."[5]

Douglas turned forty-seven as the convention began on April 23, 1860, but the delegates neither celebrated nor gave him cause to celebrate. Democrats began their meeting in a foul mood: reaching Charleston required several changes of train for delegates, who arrived to find overstuffed hotels, temperatures in the nineties, and steamy, sweaty conditions. Buchanan allegedly dispatched every federal official he could find to work against Douglas, and some anti-Douglas delegates referred darkly to his loss in the popular vote to Lincoln in the 1858 Senate election, as well as to the Little Giant's positions. By the second day, reporter Murat Halstead detected "an impression prevalent . . . that the Convention is destined to explode in a grand row." The platform committee met and, unlike its Republican counterpart, which worked speedily, spent several days fashioning three options for delegates to choose from—speaking volumes about the inability of Douglas Democrats to control their fate as well as Republicans had controlled theirs. Alabama fire-eater William L. Yancey, hoping for a split that would improve the chances of southern secession, delivered an appropriately fire-eating speech accusing Douglas and the North of assaulting southern rights. In response to Yancey's demand for a totally proslavery doctrine instead of popular sovereignty, George Pugh, a senator from Ohio and Douglas ally, rose and vowed, "Gentlemen of the South, you mistake us—you mistake us—we will not do it."[6]

Lincoln followed these events with understandable interest, given his pending trip to Decatur for the state Republican meeting. After a week of balloting in Charleston, delegates from eight southern states walked out. Lincoln expected Douglas's nomination "by what is left of the Charleston convention" and added, "All parties here dislike it. Republicans and Danites"—referring to Buchanan Democrats opposed to the Little Giant—"that he should be nominated at all; and Doug. Dem's that he should not be nominated by an undivided convention." Lincoln thought the southern delegates' departure would be "just enough to permit his nomination, and not enough to hurt much at the election. This puts the case in the hardest shape for us. But fight we must; and conquer we shall; in the end." In fact, Douglas's supporters may have hoped for a walkout to reduce opposition to him—"a little eruption, but not a great one," as Halstead said. As a prognosticator of Democratic action, despite his ability to see the other side of legal and political questions, Lincoln was no seer. But neither was Douglas: after several days of balloting, with Douglas unable to muster the needed two-thirds majority, the convention adjourned, agreeing to reconvene in Baltimore six weeks later.[7]

Time healed no wounds. They festered, then opened wider in Baltimore. Douglas even tried to withdraw, but his supporters, especially from Illinois and surrounding states, refused to let him. They increasingly resembled Republicans, declaring they had compromised enough with the South. A few southern states sent two delegations, one that had been to Charleston and one that Douglas's friends helped put together in the belief that they should replace the others who had withdrawn. Again, the Deep South bolted, with Upper South Democrats joining them. The remaining northern and border state Democrats nominated Douglas.

Having sought his party's nomination twice before, Douglas welcomed even a hollow victory. Lincoln's friends at the *Chicago Press and Tribune* merrily pointed out that the controversies over the delegations and requirement that some states vote as a unit were undemocratic, meaning "Douglas' nomination, such as it is, was a fraud." That was the least of Douglas's concerns. He hoped Lincoln's old friend Alexander Stephens, a Georgia unionist who migrated from the Whigs to the Democrats, would be his running mate. But Stephens had no interest, and in true Democratic fashion, Douglas deferred to the delegates, who looked elsewhere. When their first choice declined, they chose Herschel Johnson, a Douglas supporter and Stephens ally from Georgia. Returning home to Cincinnati, Murat Halstead sat beside a Douglas delegate who "wanted the South to be made to sweat under an Abolition President. He was glad Seward was not the Republican candidate, for he would be too easy on the South. He hoped Lincoln would make them sweat."[8]

Meanwhile, the southerners who walked out of the Democratic convention took only a short trip. At another Baltimore hall, they created what the *Press and Tribune* called "the double-headed monster." For president, they chose John Breckinridge, who had been enough of a Douglas supporter in 1856 for that branch of the party to nominate him on James Buchanan's ticket; Senator Joseph Lane of Oregon, a transplanted South Carolinian, ran for vice president. Either Breckinridge fell "prey to the lures of higher preferment held out to him by plotters against the peace of the country," as the *New York Times* put it, or he legitimately hoped to save the Union by running as a proslavery candidate. He took the Deep South's position that Congress could do nothing to stop the spread of slavery but opposed secession. "It is the game of the Southern wing to defeat an election by the people and carry it into Congress, where they think they are reasonably certain of electing Breckinridge. The Douglas men here speak openly of preferring Lincoln's election to such a result," the *Times* reported. "Yancey and other extremists are delighted at the prospect. They say that they can either elect Breckinridge in the House and thus perpetuate their control over the Government, or else elect Lincoln, which will give them an opportunity to rally the South in favor of dissolution."[9]

Republicans saw it differently, even at the *Times*. Editor Henry Raymond said, "The action of the Democracy at Baltimore seems, with reasonable diligence on the part of the Republicans, to have insured the success of the Republican ticket." Lincoln agreed but remained cautious. "I hesitate to say it, but it really appears now, as if the success of the Republican ticket is inevitable. We have no reason to doubt any of the states which voted for Frémont. Add to these, Minnesota, Pennsylvania, and New-Jersey, and the thing is done," he told Anson Henry, an old Illinois friend who had moved to Oregon. "Minnesota is as sure as such a thing can be; while the democracy are so divided between Douglas and Breckinridge in Penn. & N.J. that they are scarcely less sure. Our friends are also confident in Indiana and Illinois. I should expect the same division would give us a fair chance in Oregon." Lincoln's friends were also hopeful but guarded, with Representative Elihu Washburne writing from Washington, "The result at Baltimore is treated here as a complete disruption of the democratic party, and *I so treat it*."[10]

Adding to the work awaiting Lincoln, a new party prepared to compete for the presidency. That February, thirty former Whigs and Know-Nothings issued an address, "To the People of the United States." Declaring the need for their Constitutional Union Party, they voiced doubts that Democrats and Republicans could be "safely entrusted with the management of public affairs." They called a convention for Baltimore early that May, after the Democrats met in Charleston but before Republicans gathered in Chicago.[11]

These efforts triggered a different fight for a nomination than the one Republicans and Democrats, with their obvious front-runners, waged. In the Constitutional Union race, old Democrats fought old Whigs unhappy with the existing parties and trying to organize without an existing organization. Intending to leave politics, Senator John Crittenden declined requests that he run. Winfield Scott hoped to make up for his disastrous loss as a Whig in 1852, but that loss was enough to persuade the new party to set him aside. Another military hero, Sam Houston, wanted the nomination and drew attention: he had bounced between parties, picking up friends and enemies along the way.

One possibility seemed to be fusion with Republicans, although how they proposed to reconcile their platforms seems as unclear now as it did then. Supreme Court justice John McLean, always on the lookout for any available nomination, supposedly was in the field, but as Lincoln told Trumbull, "I do not believe he would accept it, and if he did, that fact alone, I think, would shut him out of the Chicago convention." Since some Republicans supported him, and his views fit more neatly with the former Whigs, Edward Bates harbored hopes that both parties would nominate him but then decided that McLean would be the choice. Instead, the Constitutional Unionists coalesced around John Bell, a longtime Tennessee Whig who once had been close to Andrew Jackson, broke with him, and then battled James Polk and Andrew Johnson for supremacy in their home state. Bell also had opposed the Kansas-Nebraska Act, which angered southerners, but only after several proslavery votes on it. Horace Greeley, then backing Bates for the Republican nomination but convinced that only a border state conservative could block William Henry Seward, called Bell's record "the most tangled and embarrassing to the party which shall run him for President of any man's in America."[12]

When the Constitutional Unionists met in Baltimore early in May, they knew that Democrats had adjourned without a decision and that Seward seemed likely to be the Republican choice. These steps excited their hopes for victory: they saw the possibility of attracting Republicans who found Seward too radical for their taste and perhaps whichever group of Democrats that ultimately objected to their nominee. That meant avoiding anyone controversial, which eliminated Houston and McLean. A *New York Herald* correspondent noted, "There is one set, and containing no small numbers, that seems determined to galvanize petrified whiggery; another to white-wash embalmed Americanism, and the third to unite hands with the Republicans at Chicago; the fourth to harness up a squatter sovereignty team." He regretfully predicted the probable result: "an old rusty whig fossil or an American mummy." Granting the sarcasm, the reporter proved prescient: the convention turned to Bell, aged sixty-three, and chose as his running mate Edward Everett, sixty-six, a former senator, diplomat, and Harvard president and a legendary orator, later known for delivering the unmemorable oration that Lincoln outshone at Gettysburg. The platform vowed "to *recognize* no political principle other than *the Constitution of the Country, the Union of the States, and the Enforcement of the Laws*."[13]

The Bell-Everett ticket alternately haunted Republicans and struck them as a boon. The *New York Times* played down differences with the Constitutional Union Party. "In the main their views upon the Slavery question are in harmony with those cherished by the great body of the Republicans," a *Times* editorial said. "But they deprecate what they consider the sectional character of that organization, and are very anxious to adopt some measures which will bring the border Slave States back to an active political alliance with the North," which Republicans also hoped to accomplish. Unfortunately, Republicans had no way to escape their sectional cast, despite Lincoln's glee at an unexpected irony: "It is an amusing fact, after all Douglas has said about *nationality*, and *sectionalism*, that I had more votes from the Southern section at Chicago, than he had at Baltimore! In fact, there was more of the Southern section represented at Chicago, than in the Douglas rump concern at Baltimore!!" Whether that would matter during the month leading to the election would be another issue entirely.[14]

"Justice and Fairness to All"

Once Lincoln won the nomination, whatever went on with the other parties, his most pressing business was to mend fences within his own. After the convention, Seward and Thurlow Weed were nursing their wounds and Salmon Chase was miffed in Ohio. Crucially, none of them blamed Lincoln: Seward and Weed gave Greeley more credit than he deserved and paid less attention to their own failings, while Chase fumed at the apostasy of his fellow Ohioans without pondering the impact of his radicalism and political mismanagement. But, whatever their antecedents, all of them were Republicans. They shared a vision that opposed the spread of slavery and southern power over the federal government and supported free labor. Whatever their ambitions, they wanted to stop Douglas, Breckinridge, and Bell.[15]

Sometimes with help from his managers, sometimes on his own, Lincoln threw himself into the task of unifying the party. David Davis, his chief manager at the convention, targeted their fellow ex-Whig, Weed. Joined by a congressman from New York, Elbridge Spaulding, Davis and Leonard Swett urged Weed to stop in Springfield to see Lincoln before returning home. Weed went there from Chicago and spent five hours with Lincoln. That Lincoln and Weed got along should have been no surprise: they shared a love for politics, moderation on the issues, gifts as raconteurs, and a commitment to their party. Weed left impressed with Lincoln's awareness of politics and "intuitive knowledge of human nature." For his part, Lincoln told Davis, "T. W. asked nothing of me at all. He merely seemed to desire a chance of looking at me, keeping up a show of talk while he was at it. I believe he went away satisfied." Those of Lincoln's advisers who tangled with Weed when they were Democrats were less sanguine. Judd groused, "Weed & Co. are bitter, but they cannot afford to give you the cold shoulder." Trumbull called Weed "a very shrewd, fascinating man, but I remarked to the Gentleman who spoke to me on the subject that you was too prudent & cautious a man to get complicated by promises to any body." In response, Lincoln told him, "Weed was here, and saw me; but he showed no signs whatever of the intriguer. He asked for nothing; and said N.Y. is safe, without condition."[16]

Winning over Weed was part of a campaign to soothe Seward and gain his active support. In one of the first signs, a note to Trumbull told him, "Give my respects to the Republican Senators; and especially to Mr. Hamlin, Mr. Seward, Gen. Cameron, and Mr. Wade. And to your good wife" (a reminder that Lincoln wanted no part of Mary's hard feelings toward Julia Trumbull). More critically, in conferring with Davis, Spaulding suggested assuring Seward that his supporters would have access to patronage. Davis told Lincoln, "I want you to write the letter & I will copy it—as my letter," and they did so. Thus began a curious maneuver. Under Davis's name, Lincoln wrote, "Since parting with you, I have had full, and frequent conversations with Mr. Lincoln. The substance of what he says is that he neither is nor will be, in advance of the election, committed to any man, clique, or faction; and that, in case the new administration shall devolve upon him, it will be his pleasure, and in his view, the part of duty, and wisdom, to deal fairly with all." Beyond trying to seem above the fray, Lincoln noted, "He thinks he will need the assistance of all; and that, even if he had friends to reward, or enemies to punish, as he has not, he could not afford to dispense with the best talent, nor to outrage the popular will in any locality." To Carl Schurz, Lincoln added, "I beg you to be assured that your having supported Gov. Seward, in preference to myself in the convention, is not even remembered by me for any practical purpose, or the slightest u[n]pleasant feeling. I go not back of the convention, to make distinctions among its' members; and, to the extent of our limited acquaintance, no man stands nearer my heart than yourself."[17]

Whether the problem lay with Seward, Weed, their allies, or some combination of them, Lincoln ended up repeating this refrain. After Spaulding reported further concerns, Lincoln told an intermediary, "As to our uneasy friends in New York, (if there be such) all that can be said is '*Justice and fairness to all.*' More than this has not been, and can not be, said to any." When Seward received an invitation to speak in Minnesota and Illinois Republicans begged him to visit their state, Lincoln added, "I join in the foregoing invitation; and if a compliance with it will be no inconvenience to Gov. Seward, I shall be personally much gratified to meet him here." For his part, according to Trumbull, Seward seemed supportive, and Lincoln met with him when the New Yorker came to Springfield. Indeed, Seward soon made clear to his backers that they should remain true to their party.[18]

While others helped with Seward and Weed, Lincoln personally tended to Chase. Making that task easier, Chase wanted to cultivate Lincoln and largely blamed his failure to win the nomination on another Ohio radical, Ben Wade. "It gave me great pleasure to receive yours, mistakenly dated, May 17," Lincoln replied to Chase's congratulations. "Holding myself the humblest of all whose names were before the convention, I feel in especial need of the assistance of all; and I am glad—very glad—of the indication that you stand ready." Lincoln called it "a great consolation that so nearly all of those distinguished and able men" he had defeated for the nomination were "in high position to do service in the common cause," referring to Chase serving as a governor and Seward as a U.S. senator, while Bates and Cassius Clay were private citizens. Accordingly, Chase served that cause, speaking throughout the North.[19]

Support from Bates also would benefit Lincoln, and while the new nominee had no direct involvement in obtaining it, his wise management made it possible. After the convention, Illinois Republican leaders wrote to Orville Browning, a Bates supporter until Lincoln named him an at-large delegate to the national convention. "Mr. Bates would emphatically settle the Fillmore element for us," the group told Browning, who sped to St. Louis. Bates expressed no interest in campaigning for Lincoln—after all, he had refused to leave home even to campaign for himself. But he gave Browning an endorsement letter that Republicans used to appeal to conservative Republicans and old Whigs. Bates called Lincoln a "sound and safe man. He could not be sectional if he tried."[20]

Lincoln involved himself more in pacifying Bates's backers. Schuyler Colfax, a rising young pro-Bates Republican from Indiana, wrote to the nominee, "I need not say how heartily I join with your *original* friends in their greetings to you." Lincoln shot back, "You distinguish between yourself and my *original* friends—a distinction which, by your leave, I propose to forget." He also made it a point to thank Colfax for advice on other potential supporters. When Colfax reported the latest news from Indiana and suggested that he was presumptuous, Lincoln replied that "so far from regarding it as presumptuous, I should be right glad to have one from you every mail. Bear this in mind, and act accordingly. You will readily understand and appreciate why I write only very short letters." Thus, Lincoln, in a short space, made clear his desire to be kept posted on the campaign and to keep his words from falling into the wrong set of hands or creating the wrong impression.[21]

The Organizer

While Seward, Chase, and Bates could choose whether to campaign for the party's nominee—and each did so in his own way—Lincoln had to be careful. Presidential candidates were supposed to refrain from stumping on their own behalf. That was hard for Lincoln to take, since he had been active in almost every campaign since moving to Illinois. Leaving his law practice to William Herndon during the campaign, he used the governor's office, which was vacant when the legislature was out of session, and hired a secretary, German-born journalist John Nicolay, to help sift his vast correspondence. Many of the letters requested public statements and appearances, which Lincoln found hard to decline.

But Lincoln learned why he had to say no. On August 8, he went to the state fair in Springfield. With "enthusiasm . . . beyond all bounds," members of the crowd pulled him from his carriage, carried him on their shoulders to the stand, and demanded that he speak. "This assemblage having been drawn together at the place of my residence, it appeared to be the wish of those constituting this vast assembly to see me; and it is certainly my wish to see all of you," he said, foreshadowing the tenor of his remarks en route to Washington, D.C., during the winter before his inauguration. "I appear upon the ground here at this time only for the purpose of affording myself the best opportunity of seeing you, and enabling you to see me." He also revealed surprise at his reception while trying to play it down. "I confess with gratitude, be it understood, that I did not suppose my appearance among you would create the tumult which I now witness. I am profoundly gratified for this manifestation of your feelings," he said, and then reminded the crowd of why they cheered him. "I am gratified, because it is a tribute such as can be paid to no man as a man. It is the evidence that four years from this time you will give a like manifestation to the next man who is the representative of the truth on the questions that now agitate the public," he said, building to a conclusion both eerily similar to his farewell to Springfield as president-elect and redolent of his fatalism as president. "And it is because you will then fight for this cause as you do now, or with even greater ardor than now, though I be dead and gone. I most profoundly and sincerely thank you." Then he had to escape the throng on horseback.[22]

Requests for other appearances or statements flowed into Springfield. Lincoln told the crowd at the state fair, "It has been my purpose, since I have been placed in my present position, to make no speeches," and advisers urged him not to put himself in situations where he might have to speak or explain what he said. He soon learned his lesson. To a proposal that he visit his birthplace, Lincoln replied with drollery: "You suggest that a visit to the place of my nativity might be pleasant to me. Indeed it would. But would it be safe? Would not the people Lynch me?"—and reports followed that he feared for his safety. This imbroglio helped him reject Michigan radical Zachariah Chandler's invitation to join him at a state fair and another to visit Massachusetts. Asked whether he advocated temperance or if he served liquor to the committee that notified him of his nomination, Lincoln cagily requested that his reply be confidential. Seeking to avoid antagonizing either side, he responded to the anti-liquor editor's query, "Having kept house sixteen years, and having never held the 'cup' to the lips of my friends then, my judgment was that I should not, in my new position, change my habit in this respect."[23]

Indeed, Lincoln displayed wisdom in knowing what not to say. When Joshua Giddings, an abolitionist he had admired as a fellow congressman, advised silence about what he would do if elected or about any appointments, Lincoln replied that his thoughts were "very important, and are duly appreciated by me. If I fail, it will be for lack of *ability*, and not of *purpose*." When an opponent investigated whether Lincoln visited a Know-Nothing lodge in Quincy, Illinois, Lincoln replied in detail and noted that a Douglas lieutenant had tried to spread a similar story. "And now, a word of caution," he said. "Our adversaries think they can gain a point, if they could force me to openly deny this charge, by which some degree of offence would be given to the Americans" whose votes Lincoln knew to be up for grabs. "For this reason, it must not publicly appear that I am paying any attention to the charge." He parried an abolitionist's suggestion that he attack the Fugitive Slave Law, another from a Pennsylvanian wanting more evidence of his views on the tariff, and a request that he deny ever impugning Thomas Jefferson's memory. He began a letter in answer to a claim that slavery "is a *necessity* imposed on us by the negro race" by responding that "the going many thousand miles, seizing a set of savages, bringing them here, and making slaves of them, is a *necessity* imposed on *us* by *them*, involves a species of logic to which my mind will scarcely assent" but restrained himself from mailing it. His disdain for proslavery arguments might have bothered the conservative voters he hoped to capture.[24]

Lincoln took other steps to assure that he would not be misconstrued. Wisely, he turned legal business over to Herndon, which freed Lincoln for other duties and had the added advantage of occupying Herndon, whose radicalism might hurt the party and its standard-bearer—as it did when he had found time to speak and had drawn criticism. To those seeking comments, Lincoln prepared a form response for Nicolay. "He has received others of a similar character; but he also has a greater number of the exactly opposite character. The latter class beseech him to write nothing whatever upon any point of political doctrine," Lincoln wrote. "They say his positions were well known when he was nominated, and that he must not now embarrass the canvass by undertaking to shift or modify them. He regrets that he can not oblige all, but you perceive it is impossible for him to do so."[25]

Silence clearly pained him. As a legislator, candidate for the House, two-time Senate candidate, Whig and Republican leader, and presidential aspirant, he plotted campaigns for himself and others. As a Whig, he had never benefited or suffered from a national party apparatus—indeed, its diffuseness plagued the party throughout its history. As the candidate in 1860, in a campaign less national than sectional since Republicans had no reason to plead for southern votes, he ran his first national race and with a national party. In only their second presidential campaign, they understandably might be less organized than either Democratic wing, which also could rely on federal patronage. That Republicans ran as disciplined a campaign as they did was a tribute to them but especially to Lincoln, who, as had so often been the case in the Illinois Whig Party, served as his party's unseen hand.[26]

Just as Lincoln had deployed his managers well as a candidate, he continued to do so as the nominee, as his handling of the tricky situation in Pennsylvania demonstrated. When Lincoln asked what state political boss Simon Cameron said about his chances there, Trumbull replied that his Senate colleague "does not speak as confidently of Pennsylvania as Gov. Seward does of New York. . . . It depends upon the course taken by the American element." It also depended on whether Republicans could heal divisions between Cameron and gubernatorial candidate Andrew Curtin. State party chair Alexander McClure, a Curtin ally, asked Lincoln whether David Davis and Leonard Swett might speak there. Whatever Lincoln told him has disappeared, but McClure decided against them because they "might be presumed to represent you, and with even the greatest care, might put us on the defensive in some respect." Cameron's forces disliked McClure, and Cameron ally Joseph Casey apprised Swett of plans to name a separate Republican committee to counter McClure. "I confess, I do not exactly like the attitude Cameron assumes," Swett told Lincoln, who agreed. He told Swett that the "want of confidence in their Central Com. pains me. I am afraid there is a germ of difficulty in it. . . . I would like to see you & the Judge, one or both, about that matter of your going to Pa."[27]

Although leaving details to his advisers, Lincoln set the tone. Predictably, Norman Judd preferred that Davis and Swett avoid Pennsylvania; unpredictably, Judd's ally Joseph Medill disagreed and reported rumors of McClure's corruption. Finally, Lincoln sent Davis to referee. After Davis left, Lincoln received a letter from Cameron reassuring him of Pennsylvania's support, and Davis reported the same after meeting with Cameron personally. That meeting went well: Lincoln gave Davis some of his speeches from the 1840s in support of a protective tariff, the magic issue in Pennsylvania, and his economic views reassured Cameron and other Republicans. Davis came away impressed with Cameron, and Weed reported after meeting with Cameron that the feeling was mutual. When the Pennsylvanians went ahead with plans for an additional Republican committee anyway, Judd sourly noted, "I was not mistaken in my opinion as to Casey and Cameron—Nor of the use to which they intend to put the *presence* of our friend," meaning Davis.[28]

Nor had Lincoln and Davis finished mediating in Pennsylvania. The fighting endangered Curtin's chances, and the ticket with Lincoln at the top might depend on the names below his. Both sides attacked the other in letters to Lincoln and Davis, with Lincoln explaining, "I am slow to listen to criminations among friends, and never expose their quarrels on either side. My sincere wish is that both sides will allow by-gones to be by-gones, and look to the present & future only." Worse, Buchanan's machine did its best for Breckinridge, and both Democratic tickets and the Constitutional Unionists discussed fusing in hopes of gathering all of the Republicans' opponents under one roof. Weed heard the disquieting reports, passed some of them on to Lincoln and Davis, and promised to pour in funds. He concluded, "I shall be disappointed if all the *fusion* effort between Douglas and Breckinridge, does not end in *confusion*." Eventually, Cameron supplied the good news that Lincoln would carry the state and Curtin would win in spite of himself.[29]

Lincoln found other uses for Davis. He helped smooth over differences with his cousin Henry Winter Davis, a Constitutional Unionist. A force in Maryland politics, Winter Davis, a former Whig and Know-Nothing, claimed to back John Bell, although he seemed to have begun the political migration that culminated in his position as one of Lincoln's staunchest radical Republican critics. He told his Illinois cousin, "I think the Chicago nomination a wise one under the circumstances & I earnestly trust it will be successful." But Winter Davis saw two problems: Maryland voters hated Republicans, and the Republican convention had been "supremely foolish" to approve a platform plank catering to German voters. Therefore, to help, he might speak in Pennsylvania and New Jersey.[30]

Both Davises proved helpful in ways that would have been unlikely if Henry had not trusted David and David had not been so close to Lincoln. The candidate used them wisely in Indiana. Richard

Thompson, a Whig congressional colleague from Indiana who joined Bell's party, told Lincoln that he was undecided—a signal that Lincoln might win Thompson's support with the right approach. Colfax told Lincoln, "You can write, if you ever desire it, to Winter with perfect confidence. His heart is with us." Lincoln acted accordingly, and Thompson ended up working behind the scenes for Lincoln. Thompson then helped resolve an issue in Illinois, thanks to Lincoln's adroitness at managing politics and politicians. When David Davis learned that an old Fillmore appointee in Chicago supported Lincoln, he sought approval to see him. Instead, Lincoln wrote to Thompson, an ex-Fillmore man, that "a line from you to John Wilson . . . (I guess you know him well) would fix the matter." Later, Wilson denounced Bell supporters as playing into Douglas's hands and informed Davis of Thompson's role and their hopes for Lincoln. Davis also found Wilson willing to campaign and deployed him to speak.[31]

Lincoln and Thompson appreciated each other's subtlety. Thompson told him that he argued against claims that Lincoln would be "led into ultraism by radical men, but your administration will be national. If I could succeed in fixing this influence upon their mind, I should have little difficulty." When he wanted to see Lincoln but feared his activities would become known, the candidate sent Nicolay to see Thompson. Lincoln told Thompson, "If my *record* would *hurt* any, there is no hope that it will be over-looked; so that if friends can *help* any with it, they may as well do so. Of course, due caution and circumspection, will be used." Lincoln instructed Nicolay in the form of a prose poem:

> Ascertain what he wants.
> On what subjects he would converse with me.
> And the particulars if he will give them.
> Is an interview indispensable?
> Tell him my motto is "Fairness to all,"
> But commit me to nothing.[32]

While Lincoln worked with him, Davis also served as one of Lincoln's many eyes and ears. In addition to his trip to Pennsylvania, Davis made a circuit through the East and Old Northwest. In

New York, he saw Greeley, then visited Weed and Governor Edwin D. Morgan, who chaired the Republican National Committee, in Albany. Weed took Davis with him to a meeting with Rhode Island leaders, easing their minds, and then the judge swung back through Indiana, where he conferred with Thompson and various Republican leaders. By August, Davis could tell Lincoln, "You will be elected President. There is no longer a doubt of it in my mind. The democrats have no hope, or confidence."[33]

Davis also remained Lincoln's ambassador to and for Long John Wentworth. Judd complained that "there is no need of any olive branch to him" and that "there must not be unless your truest and safest friends are to be wounded." Despite Judd's warning, Lincoln heeded Davis and saw that Wentworth received an invitation to speak at a Springfield rally. Finally, though, Davis soured on Wentworth. The radical articles that Wentworth published in the *Chicago Democrat* even endorsed Seward's "higher law" doctrine, sending shudders through conservatives such as Davis, who told Lincoln that the editorials "do us harm, great harm," and that "I have reluctantly come to the conclusion that he not only wants to beat Trumbull but also you." Lincoln knew Wentworth was beyond anyone's control, patiently waited for Davis to realize that, and otherwise ignored Wentworth's pleas for attention and Davis's requests that Lincoln notice them.[34]

While the judge remained critical to Lincoln's political operations, Davis's ally Swett also played a key role—when and where Lincoln wanted him to do so. John Shaffer, a Republican from Freeport, Illinois, had written to Swett, who told Lincoln that Illinois and Pennsylvania supporters of Seward and Cameron had been promised fair treatment if they switched to Lincoln. When Swett asked Lincoln how to respond, Lincoln replied, "I see no objection to the letter you have written to Shaffer. Send it to him, but do not let him know I have seen it; and, by a postscript, tell him to come down and see me." Lincoln intended to keep his hand in day-to-day campaign operations as much as possible, and Swett assisted him where he could do the most good.[35]

Lincoln and Swett also teamed to seek support from Whig friends who sought refuge among the Know-Nothings. They consulted on

Fillmore's onetime Buffalo postmaster, James Putnam. When Swett wrote to Putnam, Lincoln told him, "Your letter, written to go to N.Y. is long, but substantially right, I believe. You heard Weed converse with me, and you now have Putnams letter. It can not have failed to strike you that these men ask for just, the same thing—fairness, and fairness only. This, so far as in my power, they, and all others, shall have. If this suggests any modification of, or addition to, your letter, make it accordingly. Burn this, not that there is any wrong in it; but because it is best not to be known that I write at all." Fillmore supported Bell, but Putnam backed Lincoln, who was quick to compliment the ex-Know-Nothing for a speech on his behalf.[36]

For those unsure of his campaign role, Lincoln took care to tell them to keep him posted and made clear that he was well aware of what went on around him. When Trumbull reported from Washington with a variety of items, Lincoln replied, "I see by the papers this morning, that Mr. Fillmore refuses to go with us. What do the New-Yorkers at Washington think of this?" He told Trumbull what he heard from Pennsylvania, adding, "I do not remember to have heard Gen. Cameron's opinion of Penn. . . . Remembering that Peter denied his Lord with an oath, after most solemnly protesting that he never would, I will not swear I will make no committals; but I do think I will not." He also implored Trumbull, "Write me often. I look with great interest for your letters now," managing to suggest his interest in updates and assure Trumbull of his importance.[37]

Nor was Trumbull his only correspondent. Lincoln wanted Caleb Smith active in the campaign, which pleased Davis, who deemed him "the finest public speaker in the Union." Not only did Smith stump for Lincoln and become secretary of the interior for his trouble, but Lincoln thanked him for his aid at the convention, reminding him that "I am, indeed, much indebted to Indiana; and, as my home friends tell me, much to you personally. Your saying you no longer consider Indiana a doubtful state, is very gratifying. The thing starts well everywhere—too well, I almost fear, to last. But we are in, and stick or go through, must be the word." He added, "Let me hear from Indiana occasionally," and similar requests went to James Harvey, a Pennsylvania editor who became his minister to Portugal; Schurz, whose reward for campaigning was the American posting in Spain and an appointment as a general; abolitionist Cassius Clay, later Lincoln's minister to Russia; and Senator James Simmons of Rhode Island. They and others, in various ways, kept Lincoln informed—and received advice in turn.[38]

Not wanting to be only a central clearinghouse for information, Lincoln busied himself with the campaign. He helped with an official biography by the *Press and Tribune*'s John Scripps and Horace White. That caused a stir in Illinois, since Judd authorized the book as state committee chairman; Davis, a committee member, knew nothing about it; and Swett had suggested that Lincoln give the job to a New Yorker whom Weed recommended. Lincoln fretted about another campaign biography by William Dean Howells, demonstrating the care with which he approached the dissemination of his views and background. Ohio political boss Samuel Galloway's concern was that the publisher was so antislavery that he would offend conservatives. Lincoln wanted nothing to do with the document and resented that the publisher claimed that he had authorized it when he had not.[39]

The authorized biography sold widely and, through his cooperation, provided the version of Lincoln's life that he wanted known. He linked himself to average voters with his recollection that he "had an axe put into his hands at once; and from that till within his twentythird year, he was almost constantly handling that most useful instrument," splitting "the rails about which so much is being said just now, though they are far from being the first, or only rails made by A." He was self-deprecating, remembering "an early start as a hunter, which was never much improved afterwards." He diffidently showed pride in his election as militia captain in the Black Hawk War of 1832—"he has not since had any success in life which gave him so much satisfaction"—and his first legislative defeat that year marked "the only time A was ever beaten on a direct vote of the people." He tried to deflect criticism by explaining his votes on the Mexican-American War as "for all the measures in any way favorable to the officers, soldiers and their families." Also, he was one of many Whigs who backed resolutions accusing James Polk of starting the war "unnecessarily and unconstitutionally," suggesting more caution and attention to legality as president. "In 1854, his profession had almost superseded the thought of politics in his mind, when the repeal of the Missouri compromise aroused him as he had never been before," Lincoln wrote, thus making a statement about his commitment to the antislavery cause.[40]

That Lincoln followed the campaign closely through correspondence and the press is clear to anyone who reads his letters and keeps his political career in mind. On the Fourth of July, Lincoln deemed his election likely that November: "I think the chances were more than equal that we could have beaten the Democracy *united*. Divided, as it is, it's chance appears indeed very slim." Lincoln showed concern about his opposition's experience in national campaigns and awareness of his party's vulnerabilities when he added, "But great is Democracy in resources; and it may yet give it's fortunes a turn. It is under great temptation to do something but what can it do which was not thought of, and found impracticable, at Charleston and Baltimore? The signs now are that Douglas and Breckenridge will each have a ticket in every state. They are driven to this to keep up their bombastic claims of *nationality*, and to avoid the charge of *sectionalism* which they have so much lavished upon us."[41]

The Strategist as Party Leader

All of Lincoln's efforts went toward a goal that he may not have realized: establishing himself as his party's leader. Herndon thought him "bored—*bored badly*," but he found more to do than his partner realized. In a preview of his presidency, he appeared deferential to other Republicans as he sought to persuade them to do as he wished or showed that he was on top of what they were doing or should do. "The point you press—the importance of thorough organization—is felt and appreciated by our friends everywhere. And yet it involves so much more of dry, and irksome labor, that most of them shrink from it—preferring parades, and shows, and monster meetings," Lincoln told Henry Wilson, a senator from Massachusetts who was no slouch at political operations and concerned at the lack of them in his region. "I know not how this can be helped. I do what I can in my position, for organization; but it does not amount to so much as it should." He and Weed updated each other on opposing candidates. "Douglas is managing the Bell-element with great adroitness" in hopes of cutting the Republican vote and winning Kentucky, New York, and Indiana by throwing votes to Bell, Lincoln reported. "In our state we know the thing is engineered by Douglas men; and we do not believe they can make a great deal out of it," he said. While Weed expected similar efforts to fail in New York, Governor Morgan sought Lincoln's advice on how Illinois would come out—an exchange in which Lincoln displayed his interest in local developments and an awareness of how national results would affect them.[42]

Lincoln also pondered where other Republicans could do the most good. He plotted the best places to send speakers. He encouraged and implored Republicans when necessary. He became vexed over rumors that Hamlin forecast doom in his home state of Maine in correspondence with Colfax. He told Hamlin, "Such a result as you seem to have predicted in Maine, in your letter to Colfax, would, I fear, put us on the down-hill track, lose us the State elections in Pennsylvania and Indiana, and probably ruin us on the main turn in November. You must not allow it." He was especially upset because, as he told Medill, Hamlin had assured him that "all *is* safe in New England." When Elihu Washburne, whose brothers were active in Maine politics, sent a reassuring letter, Lincoln replied, "I was right glad to see it. It contains the freshest 'posting' which I now have. It relieved me some from a little anxiety I had about Maine."[43]

As the general election approached, Lincoln felt more anxiety but also pleasure and relief. The results would assure him of victory, although achieving it would be difficult, as would even reaching the White House and being inaugurated. By the next March 4, the United States had divided and Lincoln faced doubts and doubters amid concerns that he could reunite the country. During the campaign, though, he managed to introduce himself to still more Republicans who might not have known him and to make his presence felt in the campaign. The quest for victory foreshadowed what he would do after the victory.

THE MAKING OF THE PRESIDENT, 1860

During the mid-1850s, as Stephen Douglas reveled in his status as one of the country's most powerful politicians, Abraham Lincoln ruminated on their different destinies: "With me, the race of ambition has been a failure—a flat failure; with him it has been one of splendid success." Lincoln envied Douglas's success and disdained how he achieved it—his inconsistency and amorality in advocating popular sovereignty, his lack of a moral center, and his truckling to the South. While Douglas neither envied nor agreed with Lincoln but did acknowledge his abilities, Lincoln demonstrated that this respect was not quite mutual. He reportedly said that Douglas did not "tell as many lies as some men I have known. But I think he cares as little for the truth for the truth's sake as any man I ever saw."[1]

Not that Douglas spared Lincoln or the Republican Party in 1860. Breaking precedent by making campaign speeches, he claimed to avoid personal attacks, telling one crowd, "He is a very clever fellow—a kindhearted, good natured, amiable man. I have not the heart to say anything against Abe Lincoln; I have fought him so long that I have a respect for him." But Douglas's campaign reverted to the black equality arguments with which he had besmirched Lincoln in 1858. His New York supporters tossed around terms like "Nigger Equality" and designed a parade float depicting *New York Tribune* editor Horace Greeley and a black woman, whom "he caressed with all the affection of a true Republican." Douglas's allies at the *New York Herald* warned that "if Lincoln is elected you will have to compete with the labor of four million emancipated Negroes." Nor did Democrats stop there: one pro-Douglas newspaper misrepresented then-Congressman Lincoln's criticism of the Mexican-American War by telling veterans to oppose him "not only because he sought to stigmatize you as murderers, but because when you were almost reduced to starvation . . . he, with fanatics of kindred stamp, refused to promptly send you supplies" and "asks to be made president of the United States by the hands of a people he has signally outraged."[2]

Once the outcome became clear, though, Douglas acted differently than Lincoln anticipated, if his view of the Little Giant suggested any expectations at all. At a stop in Cedar Rapids, Iowa, Douglas learned that Republicans had won Pennsylvania and Indiana. He told his secretary, "Mr. Lincoln is the next President. We must try to save the union. I will go South." In doing so, Douglas upbraided fire-eaters and expressed reverence for the Union, speaking out of a combination of unionism and political opportunism. Thus, Douglas contributed to the irony of his life: no one did more than Lincoln to put himself in the White House, but the next most important person on the list may well have been Douglas.[3]

The Failure of Fusion

In retrospect, with four legitimate candidates competing—Lincoln, Douglas, John Bell, and John Breckinridge—the 1860 presidential election seems unusual. Even a prominent third-party candidate usually does little more than affect the outcome in someone else's favor. Actually, although two major parties have predominated in each presidential election, most campaigns in the quarter of a century before the voting in 1860 involved additional candidates, and the "outsider" influenced the race: antislavery candidates affected the results in 1844 and 1848, Millard Fillmore's candidacy in 1856 shaped the Republican approach to issues and voters, and the Free-Soilers in 1848 and Know-Nothings in 1856 were serious enough to have won under the right circumstances.

But the 1860 election more closely resembled what happened in 1836. At that time, the new Whig Party had doubted that it could cohere behind one nominee and defeat Democrat Martin Van Buren.

Instead, it put up a candidate for New England, another for the South, and a third for the rest of the North and West, mainly to build support at the state level. No one appears to have had it in mind at the outset, but some Whigs hoped to deprive Van Buren of enough electoral votes to throw the election into the House of Representatives, which had chosen the president in 1800 and 1824. With some of these developments within the lifetimes of many leading politicians of 1860, the possibility of lightning striking a third time seemed possible.[4]

Where that might lead was uncertain. New York radical Republican Hiram Barney was not alone in suggesting a plot to make Constitutional Union vice presidential candidate Edward Everett president through a compromise in the House. But the chances that the House could agree were dubious. It had taken weeks to choose a speaker a year before, making a battle over naming a president likely. Indeed, with each state's delegation having one vote on the president, the House was so closely divided that literally almost anything could have happened. Making matters more interesting, the Constitution mandated that the House choose from the top three in the electoral college, which—as is now known—would have eliminated Douglas, leaving his supporters up for grabs. Douglas would have fought any effort for Breckinridge, but whether he would have backed Lincoln or Bell, or even some other choice, is unknown. In turn, if the House deadlocked, the Senate would choose the vice president. Given southern dominance there, Joseph Lane, Breckinridge's running mate, would have been the likely pick.[5]

Thinking that throwing the election into the House might be the only way to defeat Lincoln, his opponents acted accordingly. That is, they tried. Douglas and Bell supporters attempted fusion in several northern areas. New York Democrats cobbled together a ticket with which they hoped to unite anti-Lincoln forces, while Constitutional Union supporters counted on the prospect of Lincoln's election to force Democrats to unify with them. In the *New York Tribune*, Greeley called it the "Confusion Ticket," and even Democrats muttered about "'fusion' (understood to mean confusion)." But the Democratic chasm proved too deep to bridge. "As to gains of democratic congressmen, if they are to be of the Douglas stripe they will be more dangerous than armed abolitionists," said John Slidell, James Buchanan's friend and ally from Louisiana. "Had I been a citizen of New York I never would have consented to a fusion which degrades sound national democrats." He saw "no appreciable difference" between Republicans and Douglas Democrats, and Douglas and his supporters felt similarly about Breckinridge and the secessionists. That was good news for Republicans, who worried—for good reason—that the Bell-Everett ticket's conservatism appealed to New York's business community.[6]

Constitutional Unionists fared little better at fusion than Democrats did. Bell concluded, "There is no probability that Douglas can be elected in any contingency likely to happen; nor can Breckinridge get a single vote North." That left the possibilities that Bell could win or the election could wind up in the House. But one of the faults of the old Whig Party—its inability to run a national campaign—proved problematic for Bell supporters who had come mainly from that organization and retained its characteristics. The Constitutional Union Party platform's intended ambiguity appealed to some but repelled others. While Bell and his followers appeared to see the dangers of southern secession more clearly than Lincoln did, they misjudged or ignored the northern sentiment moving toward Republicans.[7]

Yet hindsight demonstrates the danger Lincoln faced from fusion, the inability of fusionists to figure out how to achieve their goal, and Lincoln's good fortune that they failed. If anyone but Lincoln had won New York's thirty-five electoral votes, none of the candidates would have won a majority and the election would indeed have gone into the House. Although party leaders focused on other states, New York worried them. "I think there will be the most extraordinary effort ever made, to carry New-York for Douglas," Lincoln warned Thurlow Weed, who shared Lincoln's love for political engineering and hardly needed the warning. "You, and all others who write me from your state, think the effort can not succeed; and I hope you are right; still it will require close watching." Weed doubted both that the other parties could unite and that it would matter if they did. It did no harm to Lincoln's cause that he reached out to old Fillmore supporters, whom Douglas or a fusion ticket would need in order to stop him, and New York remained as divided as ever.[8]

The divide in New York was not unique. Hiram Barney, familiar with the issues in his bailiwick, feared "the probability of a fusion among our enemies" in the key state of Pennsylvania. But despite working hard in several states to unify Lincoln's opposition, Constitutional Unionists lamented that Republicans had little to worry about. A Bell backer in Connecticut remained convinced "that whatever differences of opinion may exist in the Dem. Ranks—and however earnest—the adherents of the two wings may appear to be,—all will be settled before the campaign has far advanced. Both sides are ready to join with us"; however, he fell short as a political prognosticator. Other New Englanders doubted that any fusion—or, for that matter, defeating Lincoln in their region—was possible.[9]

Breckinridge supporters were more rigid on slavery than Douglas Democrats, but they reversed roles on fusion, with Douglas proving unwilling to negotiate. Attending the Connecticut Democratic convention, a Constitutional Unionist found that southern sympathizers "to my surprise manifested a much more conciliatory spirit than the Douglass [sic] men," although Douglas and Bell actually discussed forming a pro-union party. John Allen, a former Whig congressman, reported from Cleveland, "The best feeling exists among the two sections of the Dem. party and the Bell men, but the democracy are exceedingly bitter toward each other and I do not think can be combined under any circumstances." In June, Breckinridge told a Democratic leader, "It is said Mr D will insist on a ticket *every where*. I deeply regret the state of things, but shall do my duty quietly and firmly." A Democratic newspaperman wrote, "I am honestly of opinion that there is a quasi coalition between the Douglas men and the Blacks," or Republicans. "I do not mean that they have yet conferred together, but that they will unite cordially and defeat Breckenridge [sic] and elect Lincoln. I have not a shadow of a doubt."[10]

How these views lacked credibility was clear when they lumped together all northerners, but Douglas was indeed determined to stop Breckinridge. During the campaign, Senator Jefferson Davis of

Mississippi, who combined a passion for southern rights with a desire for a compromise, approached Douglas with an offer: withdraw with Breckinridge and Bell in favor of a pro–southern unionist such as New York Democrat Horatio Seymour. Breckinridge and Bell apparently would go along if Douglas would, but the Little Giant refused. He reasoned that these efforts would fail anyway, and he still considered himself the only candidate who could defeat Lincoln. He acted out of selfishness or pique—or to try to save his party from a permanent rupture. He preferred losing to Lincoln to appeasing his southern enemies, and accepting Davis's proposal or any other form of fusion would legitimate Breckinridge's nomination by the alternate Democratic convention, destroying Douglas's claim to party preeminence.[11]

Some Republicans suggested that Douglas anticipated the eventual result and prepared for it. Predicting a Lincoln victory, the *New York Times* added, "We think it not . . . unlikely that Mr. Douglas himself fully shares this opinion." Massachusetts Republican Anson Burlingame recalled Douglas talking about Lane, Breckinridge's vice presidential candidate, and three Democratic enemies. "Burlingame, I am elected Senator for six years; I have got Joe Lane's head in a basket, and shall soon have [John] Slidell's, [Jesse] Bright's and [Graham] Fitch's," he said of three Buchanan allies in Congress, then marveled at "McDougal returned from California, Baker from Oregon, and Douglas and 'Old Abe,' all at Washington together—for the next President is to come from Illinois!" Douglas also reportedly told a congressman, "By God, sir, the election shall never go into the House; before it shall go into the House, I will throw it to Lincoln."[12]

Throughout the campaign, Douglas and Breckinridge did the Republican Party's job by targeting each other. Breckinridge's campaign often focused more on attacking Douglas than on winning the election. Douglas wanted to move into the White House or keep any other Democrat out of it, since either would solidify his chances of controlling the party and winning the nomination later. Buchanan and his allies tried to help Breckinridge with their control of federal patronage, depriving Douglas of potent support. But through three Senate terms and two other presidential tries, Douglas assembled a cadre of supporters, and Breckinridge had no comparable experience. Many Republican delegates whose votes helped nominate Lincoln in Chicago came to the convention backing someone else but left united behind Lincoln. By contrast, Democrats tended to be pro- or anti-Douglas, and not even united in their disunity.[13]

Douglas also violated precedent by campaigning more openly than any other presidential candidate before him. As his advisers put it, he sought to maintain control over his party, block fusion with proslavery Democrats, avert what he considered the possibility of a coup attempt, and promote popular sovereignty. He took a page from William Seward when he accused Republicans and Breckinridge Democrats of waging "an irrepressible conflict that can never be quelled until you decree that Congress shall not legislate in relation to private institutions anywhere." Criticized for campaigning—Breckinridge called him "a traveling mountebank"—he learned that northern businessmen linked to the South feared hurting their interests by donating to his campaign. Whether or not he hurt himself politically, he certainly hurt himself physically: his throat grew raw from haranguing crowds, and his increased drinking only made matters worse.[14]

While Lincoln remained interested in the campaign, his abilities as an organizer and a seer proved limited to his party; he could do little more than what he already had done. But he carefully evaluated what went on around him. He explained why he expected fusion to fail:

> I once knew a good, sound churchman, whom we'll call Brown, who was on a committee to erect a bridge over a very dangerous and rapid river. Architect after architect failed, and at last Brown said he had a friend named Jones who had built several bridges and could build this. "Let's have him in," said the committee. In came Jones. "Can you build this bridge, sir." "Yes," replied Jones, "I could build a bridge to the infernal regions, if necessary." The sober committee were horrified, but when Jones retired, Brown thought it but fair to defend his friend. "I know Jones so well," said he, "and he is so honest a man and so good

an architect that, if he states soberly and positively that he can build a bridge to hades, why, I believe it. But I have my doubts about the abutment on the infernal side." So, when politicians said they could harmonize the northern and southern wings of the Democracy, why, I believed them. But I had my doubts about the abutment on the southern side.

As it turned out, for Lincoln, building a bridge to the southern side proved far more difficult than erecting the abutment on the northern side. Among Democrats, neither side was willing enough to build—but the northern side was even less willing.[15]

The Fateful Ninth of October

As the campaign went on, Lincoln remained attentive to his fate and fusion. To a friend in Oregon, he surmised, "With the two tickets in the field I should think it possible for our friends to carry Oregon. But the general result, I think, does not depend upon Oregon. No one, this side of the mountains, pretends that any ticket can be elected by the People, unless it be ours. Hence great efforts to combine against us, are being made, which, however, as yet, have not had much success." To other allies, he expressed concerns about Pennsylvania. He told one, "You are right in the suspicion that our foes are now driving at Pennsylvania; but our friends there are fully apprized of this, and say they can and will repulse them."[16]

While Lincoln's interest in political developments belied the image of him as detached, his response to what he learned also countered the later view of him as believing, as Hamlet did, "There's a divinity that shapes our ends, / Rough-hew them how we will." By mid-September, advising national Republican chair Edwin Morgan on what was best for the party, he revealed his hopes and knowledge by writing that "in my opinion, no one thing will do us so much good in *Illinois*, as the carrying of *Indiana* at the October election. The whole surplus energy of the party throughout the nation, should be bent upon that object up to the close of that election. I should say the same of Pennsylvania, were it not that our assurances seem so abundant of Curtin's election." A week later, he allowed, "So far as

I have private information, the prospect for the election looks quite encouraging."[17]

In another encouraging sign, Seward overcame his initial disappointment to campaign. As October began, his caravan took him to Springfield, where, the *Chicago Press and Tribune* reported, "Mr. Lincoln met Mr. Seward at the train and was greeted by him in the most cordial manner, and afterwards alluded to him in his speech in highly complimentary terms, the Senator regarding his election as a foregone conclusion." Reminding Seward that they had met campaigning for Zachary Taylor in 1848, Lincoln told him, "Twelve years ago you told me that this cause would be successful, and ever since I have believed that it would be." Before a Chicago crowd, Seward struck the moderate tone Lincoln desired: "Neither you nor I have any power to disturb those of our fellow citizens in the Southern States who maintain a different system." The next day, he argued for "a National faith" based on "the principles of free soil, free labor, free speech, equal rights and universal suffrage." Although Lincoln thanked him for his comments, some of Lincoln's allies felt that Seward campaigned more for the party than for the candidate, and the eternally concerned and conservative David Davis complained that Seward invited trouble by referring to John Brown and other abolitionists.[18]

Indeed, the pending state elections loomed larger for Lincoln and his fellow Republicans than the dangers of a mere mention of Brown. Lincoln and his allies were determined that Illinoisans elect Richard Yates governor and a Republican legislature to return Lyman Trumbull to the Senate. When Joseph Medill of the *Chicago Press and Tribune* assured him of Republican strength in the state, Lincoln replied, "What you say about the Northern 30 counties of Illinois pleases me. Keep good your promise that they will give as much majority as they did for Fremont, and we will let you off. We can not be beaten, nor even hard run, in the state, if that holds true." Norman Judd, the state Republican chair and a vital cog in Lincoln's campaign for the nomination, sought funds from eastern sources. He warned, "The democracy are already importing into the doubtful districts and daily I am advised from the interior of perambulating

Irishmen in the doubtful district, seeking employment. With money we can beat this," although his New York recipient fretted about "the expensiveness of the machinery to be employed."[19]

Elsewhere, state elections would foretell the presidential results. Maine and Vermont voted in September and predictably went Republican. But Lincoln and his supporters cared far more about the voting on October 9, four weeks before the final presidential voting elsewhere, in Pennsylvania and Indiana (Ohio would vote but seemed safely Republican). "Tomorrow is the most important day in the history of the Country—as that day decides the State contests in Penn & Ind. My information received from both States is very encouraging—and yet, I shall be uneasy until the final returns are received," David Davis told his son. Secretary of the Treasury Howell Cobb wrote to his wife, "We are all looking with breathless anxiety to hear from the Pennsylvania election." James Bayard, a Delaware Democrat, admitted that "I have lost much of the confidence I felt in the defeat of Lincoln in Pennsylvania"—with good reason. Despite Republican divisions and fusion efforts, Pennsylvania elected Andrew Curtin governor by 32,000 votes, and Indiana's Republican ticket won by more than 10,000 votes.[20]

Publicly silent, Lincoln said nothing to suggest grave concerns, but his pleasure at the news and its meaning resonated in his letters and meetings with visitors. To friends gathered to check the results that night, he said, "Douglas might learn a lesson about what happens when one tries to get people opposed to slavery to vote for slavery. It is not my name, it is not my personality which has driven Douglas out of Indiana and Pennsylvania, it is the irresistible power of public opinion, which has broken with slavery." He told Seward, "It now really looks as if the Government is about to fall into our hands. Pennsylvania, Ohio, and Indiana have surpassed all expectations, even the most extravagant." To a Pennsylvania ally, he said, "We are indulging in much rejoicing over the late splendid victories in Pennsylvania, Indiana, and Ohio, which seem to foreshadow the certain success of the Republican cause in November." Mary Lincoln confessed, "I scarcely know, how I would bear up, under defeat. I trust that we will not have the trial."[21]

Lincoln's allies responded with glee, as did party faithful. Campaigning in Petersburg, Illinois, that night when a report arrived, William Herndon "opened the letter and read it over to myself . . . then I read it aloud to the crowd. I never finished that speech. The crowd yelled—screamed—threw up their hats—ran out of doors—made bonfires—&c. &c." Others in Illinois responded with similar excitement. In Springfield, Republicans gathered at the square while fireworks went off around town, then headed for Lincoln's home. He happened to be meeting with Trumbull, who told the crowd that "you have called on me to say a few words to you, instead of having called Mr. Lincoln, because you excuse him on account of his having an engagement to make a speech on the fourth of March next," inspiring further cheers.[22]

The most entertaining report on reaction came from Ward Lamon, Lincoln's friend from the legal circuit. No doubt contemplating collecting on his bets on the election inspired whimsy. He reported to Lincoln that Davis "is in a d——l of a fix." When the judge heard about Pennsylvania and Indiana, "he was trying an important commercial case, which terminated in his kicking over the clerk's desk, turned a double somersault and adjourned court until after the presidential election—and in his delirium he actually talks of Lincoln's election as being a fixed fact." So it was, although the three-hundred-pound Davis exerting himself that way was an image that even Lincoln at his most fanciful might not have conjured. But Davis revealed his and his friend's sober side when he visited a week later and found Lincoln already looking conscious of his pending responsibilities.[23]

The more realistic celebrating spread through Republican enclaves. In towns and cities from Iowa to Wisconsin and along the Pacific Coast, Republicans held meetings and parades. Their leaders, some of them Lincoln's eyes and ears in the field, provided optimistic assessments. From Pennsylvania, Alexander McClure said, "Douglasism died a natural death in this State yesterday. The organization has been dissolved and the fight abandoned." From Indiana, Mark Delahay chimed in, "There is too much of the smoke of the *battle* hovering over the field to make any accurate count of the dead. We only can report that all of the Douglas army are badly wounded," while Caleb Smith added, "Our victory is completely exceeding our most sanguine expectations." Out on the stump, Carl Schurz reported, "I feel as though I heard the cannon thunder all over the North."[24]

But the voting was far from over. Illinois received ample attention—indeed, extra attention, according to Davis, from "speakers from abroad. *Now*, that the Presidential election is settled, they wish to show their devotion & worship the rising sun. I do not envy Lincoln his eminence." Revealing its Whig antecedents by likening Lincoln's impending triumph to earlier victories by William Henry Harrison and Zachary Taylor, New York's Republican committee issued a circular crowing, "In view of results so auspicious as those which have just crowned the efforts of our Republican Friends in Pennsylvania, Indiana and Ohio, we tender you our heartfelt congratulations. Following the great and glorious triumphs in Vermont and Maine, these signal victories furnish unerring evidence that the People, weary of misrule, will, as they did in 1840, and again, in 1848, rise and reform their Government." But with the "Sham Democracy" still out in force, it warned, "No Republican should, in any manner, relax his exertions."[25]

Republicans also began looking beyond the election. Representative Elihu Washburne felt confident enough to tell Lincoln, "There seems to be but little doubt now of the result of the Presidential election," and "I am prepared to see you utterly overrun after the 6th of November, and I should feel very reluctant to be among . . . the crowd that will surround you." But he overcame his reluctance. "Yet, should it be agreeable I should like to see you. I have no axes to grind and no personal purposes to accomplish," he said. "I think my long experience in public life and my extensive knowledge of public men give me an insight into the dangers that will surround a new administration. I believe I can give you some ideas that may be useful, but I have no desire to thrust any suggestions upon you."[26]

Washburne's reluctance proved unusual: few Republicans had qualms about making suggestions to Lincoln. Turning aside pleas that, with his election certain, he should try to reassure the South, he asked a friend in New York, "What is it I could say which would quiet alarm? Is it that no interference by the government, with slaves or slavery within the states, is intended? I have said this so often already, that a repetition of it is but mockery, bearing an appearance of weakness, and cowardice, which perhaps should be avoided." The *New York Times* suggested that he would issue a statement after the election, prompting national party secretary George Fogg to counsel silence and Lincoln to tell him not to "live in much apprehension of my precipitating a letter upon the public." But when he heard rumblings that officers at Fort Kearney would "take themselves, and the arms at that point, South, for the purpose of resistance to the government," he wrote to an old friend, Major David Hunter, "While I think there are many chances to one that this is a hum-bug, it occurs to me that any real movement of this sort in the army would leak out and become known to you. In such case, if it would not be unprofessional, or dishonorable (of which you are to be judge) I shall be much obliged if you will apprize me of it," and Hunter assured him that he would do so.[27]

The Democratic reaction to the news from Pennsylvania and Indiana also demonstrated the wisdom of Lincoln's caution. Some Douglas supporters began switching to Lincoln as the only way to break the slave power, whose advocates made their displeasure evident. Far too many southerners showed that they saw Lincoln as a caricature, a fire-breathing antislavery fanatic determined to destroy their way of life. The brother of Howell Cobb, once considered a moderate, wrote of Lincoln's impending victory, "I confess it sounded to me as the death knell of the Republic. I can see no earthly hope of defeating [the Republicans] in November and their success then, whether we will it or not, is *inevitable disunion*. And calmly and coolly . . . is it not best? These people hate us, annoy us, and would have us assassinated by our slaves if they dared. . . . They are a *different* people from us. . . . Why then continue together?" These were not the sentiments of people to whom a reassuring message from Lincoln would matter.[28]

But Douglas hoped to have an impact by speaking in the South. Although he knew that the presidency lay beyond his grasp, at least for the moment, he told crowds that, if elected, he would hang secessionists "higher than Haman." His Freeport Doctrine—repudiating

Dred Scott without explicitly saying so by staying true to popular sovereignty—gave way to his Norfolk Doctrine: before a Virginia audience, he denied that southerners had the right to secede without an overt act of aggression against them. For Douglas's trouble, Breckinridge's supporters were apoplectic, and threats against Douglas's life followed. In Georgia, Alexander Stephens introduced him and asked listeners to give him "a careful, calm, and patient hearing. He comes to address not your passions, but your intellects." Ironically, Stephens soon called on Lincoln privately to repudiate the Republican platform and charged his party with aiding John Brown, which belied his call for intellect over passion and reminded Lincoln of why he had decided to maintain silence, even after his election seemed assured.[29]

Election Day

The certainty of Lincoln's election relieved some anxiety, but it did not eliminate it. David Davis still fretted about Long John Wentworth, the mercurial Chicago mayor and editor of the *Chicago Democrat*. The feuding was bad enough that when, in his official capacity, Wentworth introduced Seward, the *Press and Tribune* refused to use his name. Davis met with Wentworth "and remonstrated with him about his course, but to no purpose." He lamented, "Our party is very much demoralized here, owing to the warfare between the two papers." Meanwhile, Republicans kept campaigning hard throughout the North. While they enjoyed watching their opponents self-destruct, they took their shots at Douglas, trying to win old nativist support by accusing him of "unlimited submission to the spiritual and temporal authority of the wicked woman of Babylon." The *Press and Tribune* asked, "Is Douglas a Catholic?" and answered yes: his wife was Catholic, his sons attended a Catholic school, and he enjoyed support from Catholic voters. Taking no chances, Republicans tried to win over former Know-Nothings with reminders of Douglas's earlier opposition to Whiggery, and for temperance advocates, they pointed out that Lincoln drank no alcohol while Douglas liked it to excess.[30]

These appeals reflected what historian Richard Carwardine calls Republicans' "capacity to touch an ethical-religious nerve." For old-line Protestants concerned about the recent influx of Irish and

German Catholics, Republicans tilted just enough toward nativism to reassure them that their party was safe. When he ran for Congress in 1846, Lincoln issued a handbill denying his "infidelity," but Mary Lincoln's attendance at Springfield's Presbyterian church and Lincoln's purchase of a pew there made him look more religious than he was, at least at the time, and descriptions of his abstemious habits overcame concerns among temperance reformers about his unwillingness to try to impose them on others. Just as Whigs had been part of the evangelical Protestantism of the Second Great Awakening, Republicans positioned themselves and their antislavery ideology on the right side of "Christ's doctrine of righteousness conflicting with evil."[31]

When election day, November 6, came at last, Lincoln began it like any other day during the campaign, sitting in his statehouse office and meeting with visitors. He originally planned not to vote. Supporting himself at the ballot box would have seemed arrogant. Asked how he would vote, he said, "Well, undoubtedly like an Ohio elector of which I will tell you—by ballot." But Herndon reminded him of the rest of the ticket and said, "Lincoln you ought to go and vote." With Lamon on one side and Elmer Ellsworth, then reading law in his office, on the other, Lincoln walked to the polls with friends, including Herndon and Ozias Hatch. Republicans cheered and Democrats doffed their hats in respect. A Democrat yelled, "You ought to vote for Douglas, Uncle Abe, he has done all he could for you." As John Nicolay, Lincoln's secretary, wrote, "The Courthouse steps were thronged with people who welcomed him with immense cheering. From the time he entered the room until he cast his vote and left it, wild huzzahing, the waving of hats and all sorts of demonstrations of applause rendered all other noises insignificant and futile." In those days when parties printed tickets, Lincoln cut off the top so that he would not vote for himself, did his duty, and returned to the governor's office.[32]

For the rest of the day, Lincoln greeted visitors and commented on the election. He expressed concern about state and local candidates. He reputedly dismissed concerns about New York fusionists by suggesting "that they would probably get into such a row going up Salt

River as to 'obstruct navigation' thereafter," referring to a mythical body of water that meant total ruin. When Hatch joked about his good fortune that women lacked the right to vote, given his appearance in portraits, Lincoln replied with the story of a minister whom a church committee rejected due to a wart on his nose. He seemed relaxed, although a visitor later detected occasional twitching that suggested nervousness.[33]

That night, Lincoln awaited the returns with other Republicans at the telegraph office in Capitol Square. Watching him "chatting with three or four friends as calmly and as amiably as if he had started on a picnic," a reporter marveled that the news was "Greek to me . . . but Mr. Lincoln seemed to understand their bearing on the general result in the State and commented upon every return by way of comparison with previous elections. He understood at a glance whether it was a loss or gain to his party." Simon Cameron wired, "Pennsylvania 70,000 for you. New York safe. Glory enough." Lincoln noted, "The news would come quick enough if it was good, and if bad, I am not in any hurry to hear it." Although he had gone home earlier for dinner, he joined Republicans across the square for a meal that local women prepared at Watson's "ice cream saloon," "manufacturers and dealers in Candies, Confectionary, Fruits, etc." (although the *New York Times* reported that he ate at a local hotel, perhaps to avoid concerns about explaining that it was not an actual saloon). The women called, "How do you do, Mr. President?" Before the meal ended, a telegram from New York party leader Simeon Draper announced that his state's electoral vote seemed headed his way. "You're elected now! It's all over!" the other diners yelled. Conscious of Democratic New York City as well as other spots still not heard from, Lincoln replied, "Not too fast, my friends. Not too fast, it may not be over yet." Lincoln and his allies returned to the telegraph office until after midnight. Losing his usual reserve, Trumbull announced, "Uncle Abe, you're the next President, and I know it." Jesse Dubois led the group in a campaign song, "Ain't You Glad You Jined the Republicans?"[34]

Lincoln obviously was pleased and trying not to show it, then or afterward. His one show of emotion came when he learned that he carried Springfield and cheered the news, although he was disappointed to learn that Douglas carried the county, Sangamon. The rest of Springfield was less restrained, with cannons fired and church bells ringing throughout the night. One resident recalled the town as "perfectly wild: the republicans were singing, yelling shouting! Old men, young, middle-aged, clergymen and all!" Lincoln told the men around him, "I guess there's a little lady at home who would like to hear this news." Accounts differ, but that "little lady" allegedly had told her husband to be home by ten o'clock or she would lock him out. If so, she heard crowds rampaging through Springfield and relented, but another version described her as asleep, and he awoke her to tell her the news.[35]

Although Judd described him as "prudent, and unterrified by all the noise and bluster," Lincoln grasped that great responsibilities awaited him. He later said, "I went home, but not to get much sleep, for I then felt as I never had before, the responsibility that was upon me." He wrote down the names of the Republicans he wanted in his cabinet: Seward, Edward Bates, Salmon Chase, Gideon Welles of Connecticut, Montgomery Blair of Maryland, William Dayton of New Jersey, and Norman Judd, who chaired the Illinois state party—and, incredibly, all but Dayton and Judd became cabinet members, and the two of them received diplomatic posts. The next day, he greeted reporters by saying, "Well, boys, your troubles are over, mine have just commenced." Other Republicans expressed similar sentiments. Fogg wrote, "The deed is done. The victory of Republicanism over slave Democracy is won. The friends of constitutional liberty—of 'free speech, free labor, a free country, and free men'—have triumphed. To your hands are entrusted the destinies of the most important revolution of modern times," while Chase chimed in from Ohio, "The space is now clear for the establishment of the policy of Freedom on safe & firm grounds. The lead is yours. The responsibility is vast."[36]

Lincoln went to work on two fronts: planning for his presidency and avoiding any public statement about the South. For the former, he wrote to vice president–elect Hannibal Hamlin, "I am anxious for a personal interview with you at as early a day as possible. Can you, without much inconvenience, meet me at Chicago?" He had received a memorandum from General Winfield Scott briefing him on possible secession and suggesting policies that Lincoln would largely ignore. Lincoln waited ten days—until after the election—to write back to thank him for his views "and especially for this renewed manifestation of his patriotic purposes as a citizen, connected, as it is, with his high official position, and most distinguished character, as a military captain." When another old Whig, former party leader Truman Smith, suggested a post-election bow toward the South, Lincoln's response set the tone for the ensuing months. "I could say nothing which I have not already said, and which is in print, and open for the inspection of all. To press a repetition of this upon those who have listened, is useless," he concluded, and "to press it upon those who have refused to listen, and still refuse, would be wanting in self-respect, and would have an appearance of sycophancy and timidity, which would excite the contempt of good men, and encourage bad ones to clamor the more loudly."[37]

Why Lincoln Won

Lincoln's victory was both limited and large. He easily won the electoral college, earning 180 votes—all of the North and West except New Jersey, which he split with Douglas, and his native Kentucky, which went for Bell. Republicans blamed the divide in New Jersey on the lack of support Lincoln received from the still-Whiggish Dayton and Speaker of the House William Pennington. *New York Evening Post* editor John Bigelow groused, "That little State, the property of a railroad company [the Camden and Amboy] which runs through it and twirls it around like a Skewer voted against him because it had misfortune to be inhabited by two men, each of whom wished to be Secretary of the Navy and hoped by making the State look insecure, to get an offer of terms"—and, ironically, Lincoln sent Dayton to Paris as minister to France, with Bigelow as his assistant.[38]

The size of Lincoln's victory depends on how it is analyzed. Historians have debated whether fusion or the swing of a few thousand votes could have changed the outcome. In almost every state he carried, Lincoln won an outright majority. In Illinois, he captured

50.7 percent of the vote to Douglas's 47.2—any which way, a massive repudiation of Buchanan and an outpouring for two favorite sons. He won majorities in New York, New Jersey, and Rhode Island against full or partial fusion tickets. In addition to South Carolina, where direct democracy of any kind remained anathema, Lincoln's name was absent from the ballot across the South: Alabama, Arkansas, Florida, Georgia, Louisiana, Mississippi, North Carolina, Tennessee, and Texas. Douglas won one other state, Missouri, a border slave state. Bell ran fewer than 500 votes behind Douglas there and carried Kentucky easily, his native Tennessee comfortably, and Virginia barely. In each Bell state, the runner-up was Breckinridge, who swept the Deep South and the middle ground of Maryland (barely) and Delaware (easily). Only in California, where Lincoln won with 32.3 percent, and in Buchanan's Pennsylvania did Breckinridge make any kind of showing in the North.[39]

That the country was bitterly divided was both true and false. Nearly 60 percent of the popular vote went to the proslavery (Breckinridge) or antislavery (Lincoln) candidate, with the rest to Douglas and Bell, the unionists who wanted to calm the debate. The number of northerners for Breckinridge was minuscule, and the number of southerners for Lincoln probably would not have filled any self-respecting tavern. The South was more divided than the North over slavery: while northerners resentful of southern power wanted to stop its spread or have a say in the decision, southern voters proved less certain. While Breckinridge and Bell split the South, the combined votes of Bell and Douglas topped Breckinridge's in the slave states, suggesting some sentiment for a compromise or at least a conservative approach to sectional differences. Further, if fusion had spread across the North, the number of electoral votes affected—perhaps a dozen—would have been too little to derail Lincoln, unless fusion had suddenly become popular in such large states as New York and Pennsylvania.[40]

The West Coast provided an unusual twist on Lincoln's election. In California and Oregon, he benefited from deep divisions among Democrats and the presence of his old Illinois friend Edward Baker, who stumped for him, and for himself for an Oregon Senate seat.

Lincoln won California's four electoral votes by a whisker, topping Douglas by just over 700 votes and Breckinridge by almost 5,000 out of nearly 120,000 cast. The Republican state platform ignored slavery and urged "all the opponents of the present corrupt administration to join with us in hurling it from power." The national platform's Whiggish tint on issues like the tariff mattered less to Californians than Republican support for a transcontinental railroad. In both states, the national Democratic split loomed large. California's leading Douglas supporter, Senator David Broderick, had died in a duel late in 1859 with David Terry, a southern Democrat whose allies cast their lot with Buchanan and supported the spread of slavery. In Oregon, Democrats split and the Douglas supporters made an alliance with Republicans on the state's two Senate seats. Even Breckinridge's running mate, Oregon's Joseph Lane, predicted that Lincoln would win his state, and he was right: Lincoln captured Oregon's three electoral votes by about 250 votes over Breckinridge.[41]

Whatever happened in individual states, Lincoln's victory has become mythic in its own right. He received the smallest popular vote percentage of any president since the beginning of party politics; John Quincy Adams fared worse, but in 1824, the number of votes and voters was much more limited. Yet Lincoln won a clear electoral majority, and whether a unified opposition could have beaten him is as unlikely as it is unprovable. All of which leaves the question of why he won.

A key factor in Lincoln's favor was a group called the Wide-Awakes. Each of the four candidates had his own band of supporters, but the Little Giants and Hickory Clubs paled in comparison with the Republican group, and Thurlow Weed's *Albany Evening Journal* captured a Constitutional Union gathering and torchlight parade when it said, "The meeting was slim and highly respectable, the procession highly respectable, but slim. . . . All that was lacking was enthusiasm." For Lincoln, the Wide-Awakes received help from women holding banners announcing, "Westward the star of Empire takes its way, / We link-on to Lincoln, as our mothers did to Clay." The clubs hauled out fence rails and flagpoles, lit bonfires, and paraded by torchlight in towns across the North. Estimated to number about

100,000, they wore uniforms and resembled a political militia, ready to fight for their candidate and exciting participation and involvement among younger voters that might not have happened without the Wide-Awakes.[42]

Although some Republicans fretted about the lack of elite involvement in the Wide-Awakes and their militaristic bent, their youth contributed to Lincoln's success. "The reason we didn't get an honest President in 1856, was because the old men of the last generation were not Wide-Awake, and the young men of this generation hadn't got their eyes open," Seward, who failed to notice the irony that he was almost sixty, said before a rally of 3,000 Wide-Awakes in Detroit. "Now the old men are folding their arms and going to sleep, and the young men through the land are Wide Awake." When the *Albany Evening Journal* made the Bell-Everett party seem, as Weed's erstwhile ally Greeley put it, like "a fossil dug up from the remains of a past age. It belongs to the year 1830, and not the times in which we live," it fit a pattern of describing Constitutional Unionists, fairly or not, as relics. While the membership was more varied, their leaders were aged for that era, and their attitudes urged the country to return to when slavery was less debated, political parties were less democratic and rambunctious, and candidates supposedly espoused the ideals of virtue and deference. By contrast, Douglas had seemingly been around forever but remained youthful and boisterous, and Breckinridge was the youngest vice president ever at thirty-five and would have been the youngest man ever elected president at thirty-nine. At age fifty-one, a strong physical specimen whose image as "Honest Old Abe" made him seem more wizened and experienced than he was, Lincoln struck a happy medium.[43]

Horace Greeley also contributed to the result. Whether he would have backed a Seward ticket can only be conjectured, and he left Chicago still convinced that Bates's nomination "would have been more far-sighted, more courageous, more magnanimous"—and more contradictory, since Bates was in his late sixties and dallied with the Constitutional Unionists. But Greeley believed in two causes: the Republicans and their desire to stop the spread of slavery, and his own, which was to replace Seward in the Senate when the legislature met in 1861. Accordingly, he raised money, organized speakers, campaigned for Lincoln, published campaign documents, and kept the *Tribune*'s widely read reporting and editorial resources focused on electing a Republican slate.[44]

Clearly, and only as a last resort, Douglas helped elect Lincoln. Had Douglas accepted a southern platform as the price of Democratic unity, he would have lost some of his northern support, and insisting on popular sovereignty cost him the South, so he probably would have lost anyway. But when he rejected fusion, he doomed himself, southern Democrats, and Constitutional Unionists to defeat. He also changed the Republican outlook. A month before the Chicago convention, Greeley wrote, "I want to succeed this time, yet I know the country is not Anti-Slavery. It will only swallow a little Anti-Slavery in a great deal of sweetening. An Anti-Slavery man *per se* cannot be elected; but a Tariff, River-and-Harbor, Pacific Railroad, Free-Homestead man *may* succeed *although* he is Anti-Slavery." Democratic divisions turned the antislavery portion of the electorate into the dominant one, making Lincoln's nomination especially felicitous. Slavery mattered more to Lincoln than any of the other issues Greeley named, but he also fit the description that Greeley laid out for an ideal Republican candidate.[45]

Blissful ignorance also benefited Lincoln. His party and the North doubted that their actions or election would divide the Union, as southerners threatened. John Underwood, whom Virginians had driven from their state over his abolitionism, predicted that once a Republican took office, "Slaveholding gentlemen will cross the Potomac in swarms, and clamor at the Capitol for the privilege of serving their country in public office—Slavery or no Slavery." Arguing, "The people of the South have too much good sense, and good temper, to attempt the ruin of the government," Lincoln agreed, telling an Ohio journalist, "They won't give up the offices. Were it believed that vacant places could be had at the North Pole, the road there would be lined with dead Virginians." Northerners had listened to southerners talk for decades and had seen no action and expected none this time, either. Their misjudgment of southern plans made it easier for them to elect the candidate who most threatened the South and to ignore warnings from Breckinridge supporters in particular about the possibility of disunion. The unionist tickets also ran stronger in the cities, and the seemingly more ideological candidates—Lincoln and Breckinridge—did better in rural areas. Granting that southerners huffed and puffed over secession, the most widely disseminated news and commentary appeared in cities, which promoted the value of preserving the Union and its likely survival. Also, that huffing and puffing may have inspired some northerners to support Lincoln for the sake of teaching the South the lesson that its power over the electoral process and the government it produced could not last forever.[46]

If northerners doubted the importance of the fire-eaters to the South, the most ardent northerners played a different role. Abolitionists, best described as the Republican fringe, actually may have helped Lincoln. Lincoln apparently told Illinois abolitionist Wait Talcott, "I know you Talcotts are all strong abolitionists, and while I have had to be very careful in what I said I want you to understand that your opinions and wishes have produced a much stronger impression on my mind than you may think." Abolitionists certainly had their doubts about that, with Wendell Phillips, one of the most famous and eloquent of their number, blasting Lincoln over his willingness to enforce the Fugitive Slave Law and doubting his sincerity in drafting a bill as a congressman to end slavery in Washington, D.C. Other abolitionists and radical Republicans defended Lincoln, seeing him—correctly—as the most antislavery candidate they could hope to put in the White House. But it probably did him no harm with undecided or more conservative voters that Phillips and some of his followers attacked Lincoln.[47]

Lincoln and his party also managed the impressive feat of balancing old Know-Nothings and the immigrants they opposed. Increasing Republican tallies by 120,000 in Pennsylvania, 30,000 in New Jersey, 45,000 in Indiana, and 76,000 in Illinois, Lincoln gained support in the states that had gone Democratic and cost his party the presidency in 1856. He drew so well from Americans who had backed Fillmore that Herndon wrote to Charles Sumner a month after the nomination that "we are fast gaining ground out West:

the 'old line Whigs' are fast coming out for us—are going almost unanimously and wildly for Lincoln." While many of them had preferred Douglas in the Senate race in 1858, they grew to see Lincoln as moderate enough on slavery to receive their votes, however negligible the difference between his "house divided" and the presumably more radical Seward's "irrepressible conflict." Elsewhere in the North, old Whigs who migrated to the Republican Party—for example, Tom Corwin and Tom Ewing, long active in Ohio politics, and Daniel Ullmann and Hamilton Fish in New York—supported him. He polled 500,000 votes more than John C. Frémont had in 1856, and while Fillmore had won 395,000 northern votes, Bell could carry only 78,000, prompting some Constitutional Unionists to lament their inability to persuade Kentucky's John Crittenden to seek the nomination. Even efforts to link Lincoln to nativism did nothing to cut substantially into his support among German-American voters.[48]

All in all, though, Lincoln's greatest asset was himself. Some of his characteristics—who he was, not whom he represented or who others believed him to be—helped elect him. His background exemplified the equal opportunity and social mobility that northerners believed to be true of their society and nonexistent in the South. His reputation for honesty contrasted starkly with the reports of corruption that tainted Buchanan's administration and made him more appealing as a candidate than Seward, whose ties to Weed blemished him. His ability to be antislavery without being critical of the South or threatening to conservative northerners positioned him perfectly on the political spectrum for the nomination and the election—and, subsequently, his presidency.

In addition to benefiting from his reputation and image, Lincoln demonstrated deftness as a political manager. He managed the proceedings that led to his unified support in Illinois, stamping him as different from Seward, whose New York delegation's unanimity was illusory, and from Chase, whose Ohioans did little to help him. Lincoln placed the right people in Chicago to help him win the nomination. During the campaign, he made overtures to those who could best help him, avoided those who would do him no good, involved himself when he knew he could benefit, and distanced himself when that approach would be to his advantage. That he managed this so adroitly and successfully was no surprise to Illinois politicians who knew him or of him. Soon, the rest of the country would find out what the Illinoisans already knew.

According to his friend Ward Lamon, from "boyhood up," Lincoln confessed, "my ambition was to be President." Publicly, he long had made clear that was beyond possibility or imagining and even claimed to the end of his campaign that he would have preferred simply to have won election to the Senate in 1858. Privately, not only did he dream of the presidency, but he also did all he could to make the dream a reality. The 1860 election changed the country: six weeks after Lincoln's election, South Carolina seceded from the Union, and almost six weeks after he took office, the firing on Fort Sumter began the war that ended slavery, established that the United States was indeed a nation, and elevated Lincoln to martyrdom. Whatever might have happened with a different candidate and victor, this much is clear: no one did more than Abraham Lincoln to make sure that *he* would be that candidate and victor, and the ability that he demonstrated in the process prepared him to lead the North to victory in the Civil War.[49]

NOTES

INDEX

NOTES

1. Prelude to a Turning Point

1. Harold Holzer, *Lincoln President-Elect: Abraham Lincoln and the Great Secession Winter, 1860–1861* (New York: Simon and Schuster, 2008), 45.

2. Eric Foner, *The Story of American Freedom* (New York: W. W. Norton, 1998), 35–36; Don E. Fehrenbacher and Ward McAfee, *The Slaveholding Republic: An Account of the United States Government's Relations to Slavery* (New York: Oxford University Press, 2001), 38.

3. Stanley M. Elkins and Eric L. McKitrick, *The Age of Federalism: The Early American Republic, 1788–1800* (New York: Oxford University Press, 1993), 754.

4. Thomas Jefferson to John Holmes, Monticello, April 22, 1820, in *Jefferson: Writings*, ed. Merrill D. Peterson (New York: Library of America, 1984), 1434; Daniel Walker Howe, *What Hath God Wrought: The Transformation of America, 1815–1848* (New York: Oxford University Press, 2007), 148–49.

5. Arthur M. Schlesinger Jr., *The Age of Jackson* (Boston: Little, Brown, 1946), 29.

6. Richard Hofstadter, *The Idea of a Party System: The Rise of Legitimate Opposition in the United States, 1780–1840* (Berkeley: University of California Press, 1969), 216.

7. *Illinois Gazette*, August 15, 1846, in *The Collected Works of Abraham Lincoln*, ed. Roy P. Basler (hereafter *Collected Works*), 9 vols. (New Brunswick, N.J.: Rutgers University Press, 1953–55), 1:382–83.

8. Lincoln, "To the People of Sangamo County," March 9, 1832, in *Sangamo Journal*, March 15, 1832, in ibid., 1:5–6.

9. Abraham Lincoln to Jesse Lynch, Washington, April 10, 1848, in ibid., 1:463.

10. "Address Before the Young Men's Lyceum of Springfield, Illinois," January 27, 1838, in *Sangamo Journal*, February 3, 1838, in ibid., 1:108–15; "Protest in Illinois Legislature on Slavery," March 3, 1837, *House Journal*, 10th General Assembly, 1st sess., pp. 817–18, in ibid., 1:74–75.

11. Lincoln to Williamson Durley, Springfield, October 3, 1845, in ibid., 1:347–48.

12. *Illinois Weekly Journal*, July 21, 1852, in ibid., 2:121–32.

13. Lincoln to Joshua Speed, Springfield, August 24, 1855, in ibid., 2:320–23.

14. *Illinois Journal*, October 21–28, 1854, in ibid., 2:247–83, at 248.

15. Tyler G. Anbinder, *Nativism and Slavery: The Northern Know Nothings and the Politics of the 1850s* (New York: Oxford University Press, 1992), 210–15, 235–36.

16. *Illinois State Journal*, June 18, 1858, in *Collected Works*, 2:461–69.

17. Lincoln's original spelling and punctuation have been reproduced here. Lincoln to Lyman Trumbull, Bloomington, December 28, 1857, in ibid., 2:430; Allen C. Guelzo, *Lincoln and Douglas: The Debates That Defined America* (New York: Simon and Schuster, 2008), especially 47–64.

18. Guelzo, *Lincoln and Douglas*, 191–92; Lincoln, "First Debate with Stephen A. Douglas at Ottawa, Illinois," August 21, 1858, in *Collected Works*, 3:16.

2. Tasting a Candidacy

1. William C. Harris, *Lincoln's Rise to the Presidency* (Lawrence: University Press of Kansas, 2006), 151–52; Michael Burlingame, *Abraham Lincoln: A Life*, 2 vols. (Baltimore: Johns Hopkins University Press, 2008), 1:558.

2. Abraham Lincoln to Thomas J. Pickett, Springfield, April 16, 1859, in *The Collected Works of Abraham Lincoln*, ed. Roy P. Basler (hereafter *Collected Works*), 9 vols. (New Brunswick, N.J.: Rutgers University Press, 1953–55), 3:377; Harris, *Lincoln's Rise to the Presidency*, 151–52; Richard Carwardine, *Lincoln* (London: Pearson, 2003), 91–92.

3. Lincoln to Lyman Trumbull, Springfield, April 29, 1860, in *Collected Works*, 4:45; David Herbert Donald, *"We Are Lincoln Men": Abraham Lincoln and His Friends* (New York: Simon and Schuster, 2003), xiv; William H. Herndon and Jesse W. Weik, *Herndon's Lincoln: The True Story of a Great Life*, 3 vols. (Chicago: Belford, Clarke, 1889), 2:375; Gary Ecelbarger, *The Great Comeback: How Abraham Lincoln Beat the Odds to Win the 1860 Republican Nomination* (New York: St. Martin's Press, 2008).

4. Harold Holzer, *Lincoln at Cooper Union: The Speech That Made Abraham Lincoln President* (New York: Simon and Schuster, 2004).

5. Gideon Welles, *Lincoln and Seward: Remarks Upon the Memorial Address of Chas. Francis Adams, on the Late Wm. H. Seward . . .* (New York: Sheldon & Co., 1874), 23.

6. *The Works of William H. Seward*, ed. George E. Baker, 5 vols. (Boston: Houghton Mifflin, 1884), 3:301; 4:110-11.

7. *New-York Daily Times*, February 7, 1855; *Appendix to the Congressional Globe*, 31st Cong., 1st sess., March 11, 1850, 260–69; "The Irrepressible Conflict, Rochester, October 25, 1858," in *Works of William H. Seward*, 4:289–302; Eric Foner, *Free Soil, Free Labor, Free Men: The Ideology of the Republican Party before the Civil War*, 2nd ed. (New York: Oxford University Press, 1995), 40–41.

8. *Congressional Globe*, 36th Cong., 1st sess., February 29, 1860, 910–14.

9. Foner, *Free Soil, Free Labor, Free Men*, 73–77.

10. Carl Schurz, *The Reminiscences of Carl Schurz*, 3 vols. (New York: McClure Publishing, 1907–08), 2:169–72.

11. Franklin A. Dick to Isaac Sherman, St. Louis, February 2, 1860, 1857–March 1860, Sherman Papers, Henry E. Huntington Library, San Marino, California.

12. Diary of John Quincy Adams, March 14, 1833, quoted in William E. Gienapp, *The Origins of the Republican Party, 1852–1856* (New York: Oxford University Press, 1987), 312.

13. Richard Hofstadter, *The American Political Tradition and the Men Who Made It* (New York: Alfred A. Knopf, 1948), 92–134.

14. David Herbert Donald, *Lincoln* (New York: Simon and Schuster, 1995), 232; Lincoln to W. H. Wells, Springfield, January 8, 1859, in *Collected Works*, 3:349; Lincoln to Mark W. Delahay, Springfield, May 14, 1859, in *Collected Works*, 3:379; Lincoln to Anson S. Miller, Springfield, November 19, 1858, in *Collected Works*, 3:340; Lincoln to Trumbull, Springfield, December 11, 1858, in *Collected Works*, 345.

15. Lincoln to Salmon P. Chase, Springfield, June 9, 1859, in *Collected Works*, 3:384; Lincoln to Chase, Springfield, June 20, 1859, in ibid., 3:386; Lincoln to Schuyler Colfax, Springfield, July 6, 1859, in ibid., 3:390–91.

16. Don E. Fehrenbacher, *Prelude to Greatness: Lincoln in the 1850s* (Stanford: Stanford University Press, 1962), 143; Lincoln to Dr. Anson S. Henry, Springfield, November 19, 1858, in *Collected Works*, 3:339; Harris, *Lincoln's Rise to the Presidency*, 153; David J. LeRoy, *Mr. Lincoln's Book: Publishing the Lincoln-Douglas Debates with a Census of Signed Copies* (New Castle: Oak Knoll Press, 2009).

17. Lincoln to Theodore Canisius, Springfield, May 17, 1859, in *Collected Works*, 3:380; Burlingame, *Abraham Lincoln*, 1:563–64.

18. Lincoln to Henry L. Pierce and Others, Springfield, April 6, 1859, in *Collected Works*, 3:374–76.

19. Lincoln, "Speech at Columbus, Ohio," September 16, 1859, in *Illinois State Journal*, September 24, 1859, in ibid., 3:400–425, at 405, 404.

20. Lincoln, "Speech at Cincinnati, Ohio," September 17, 1859, in *Illinois State Journal*, October 7, 1859, in ibid., 3:438–62, at 446, 453.

21. Ibid., 3:459; Lincoln, "Speech at Indianapolis, Indiana," September 19, 1859, in *Indianapolis Atlas*, September 19, 1859, in ibid., 3:463–70; Lincoln, "Address before the Wisconsin State Agricultural Society, Milwaukee, Wisconsin," September 30, 1859, in *Milwaukee Sentinel* and *Chicago Press and Tribune*, October 1, 1859, in ibid., 3:471–82, at 479.

22. Lincoln, "Speech at Elwood, Kansas," December 1, 1859, in *Elwood Free Press*, December 3, 1859, in ibid., 3:495–97; Lincoln, "Remarks upon Arriving at Leavenworth, Kansas," December 3, 1859, in *Leavenworth Times*, December 5, 1859, in ibid., 3:497; Lincoln, "Speech at Leavenworth, Kansas," December 3, 1859, in *Illinois State Journal*, December 12, 1859, in ibid., 497–502.

23. Holzer, *Lincoln at Cooper Union*. Like Holzer, I refer to the location by its better-known name, although in 1860 it was known as the Cooper Institute.

24. Lincoln, "Address at Cooper Institute, New York City," February 27, 1860, in *The Address of the Hon. Abraham Lincoln, in [V]indication of the Policy of the Framers of the Constitution and the Principles of the Republican Party, Delivered at Cooper Institute, February 27th, 1860*, Issued by the Young Men's Republican Union (New York: George F. Nesbitt & Co., Printers and Stationers, 1860), in *Collected Works*, 3:522–50, at 522, 537, 547–48, 550.

25. Lincoln to Trumbull, Springfield, February 3, 1859, in *Collected Works*, 3:355, and April 29, 1860, 4:46; Fehrenbacher, *Prelude to Greatness*, 151–53; Ralph J. Roske, *His Own Counsel: The Life and Times of Lyman Trumbull* (Reno: University of Nevada Press, 1979), 54–56; Burlingame, *Abraham Lincoln*, 1:562–63.

26. Donald, *"We Are Lincoln Men,"* xiv; Donald, *Lincoln*, 242.

27. Reinhard H. Luthin, *The First Lincoln Campaign* (Cambridge: Harvard University Press, 1944), 73–74.

28. Lincoln to Norman B. Judd, Springfield, December 9, 1859, in *Collected Works*, 3:505; December 14, 1859, 3:509; and February 5, 1860, 3:516; Lincoln to the Editor of the *Central Transcript*, Springfield, July 3, 1859, in *Collected Works*, 3:389–90; Ecelbarger, *Great Comeback*, especially 123–26.

29. Lincoln to Jesse W. Fell, Springfield, December 20, 1859, in *Collected Works*, 3:511–12; Donald, *Lincoln*, 237.

30. *New York Weekly Tribune*, April 14, 1860, in Gerald M. Capers, *Stephen A. Douglas: Defender of the Union* (Boston: Little, Brown, 1959), 201.

31. Roy F. Nichols, *The Disruption of American Democracy* (New York: Free Press, 1948), 278; William M. Browne to Samuel L. M. Barlow, Office of the "Constitution," Washington, D.C., June 29, 1860, box 31, 1860, A-B, Barlow Papers, Henry E. Huntington Library, San Marino, California; William C. Davis, *The Union That Shaped the Confederacy: Robert Toombs and Alexander H. Stephens* (Lawrence: University Press of Kansas, 2001).

32. Allen C. Guelzo, *Lincoln and Douglas: The Debates That Defined America* (New York: Simon and Schuster, 2008), 75; William Lee Miller, *Lincoln's Virtues: An Ethical Biography* (New York: Alfred A. Knopf, 2002), 397.

33. John W. Allen to John A. Rockwell, Columbus, January 7, 1860, box 35, August 1859–April 1860, Rockwell Collection, Henry E. Huntington Library, San Marino, California; Elbert B. Smith, *Francis Preston Blair* (New York: Free Press, 1980), 258.

34. Washington Hunt to John A. Rockwell, Lockport, May 19, 1860, box 36, May–September 1860, Rockwell Collection.

35. Arthur M. Schlesinger Jr., *The Age of Jackson* (Boston: Little, Brown, 1946), 49.

3. Everybody's Second Choice

1. Lincoln to Samuel Galloway, Chicago, March 24, 1860, in *The Collected Works of Abraham Lincoln*, ed. Roy P. Basler (hereafter *Collected Works*), 9 vols. (New Brunswick, N.J.: Rutgers University Press, 1953–55), 4:33–34; Lincoln to James F. Babcock, Springfield, April 14, 1860, in ibid., 4:43.

2. David Davis to Lincoln, Urbana, April 23, 1860, and Danville, May 5, 1860, Abraham Lincoln Papers, Library of Congress (hereafter Lincoln Papers, LC), Series 1, General Correspondence, 1833–1916, downloaded from http://memory.loc.gov; Gary Ecelbarger, *The Great Comeback: How Abraham Lincoln Beat the Odds to Win the 1860 Republican Nomination* (New York: St. Martin's Press, 2008), 160–65; David Donald, *Lincoln's Herndon: A Biography* (New York: Alfred A. Knopf, 1948), 135–36.

3. Lyman Trumbull to Lincoln, Washington, April 24, 1860, Lincoln Papers, LC.

4. Ecelbarger, *Great Comeback*, 166–68; *Illinois State Register*, April 17, 1860, in *Collected Works*, 4:41–42; Roy F. Nichols and Philip S. Klein, "Election of 1856," in *History of American Presidential Elections: 1789–1968*, ed. Arthur M. Schlesinger Jr. and Fred L. Israel, 4 vols. (New York: Chelsea House Publishers, 1971), 2:1040.

5. Lincoln to Richard M. Corwine, Springfield, April 6, 1860, in *Collected Works*, 4:36; Lincoln to Trumbull, Springfield, April 7, 1860, in ibid., 4:40.

6. Lincoln to Corwine, Springfield, May 2, 1860, in ibid., 4:47–48.

7. Lincoln to Norman Judd, Springfield, February 9, 1860, in ibid., 3:517; Ecelbarger, *Great Comeback*, 123–26.

8. Reinhard H. Luthin, *The First Lincoln Campaign* (Cambridge: Harvard University Press, 1944), 48; William C. Harris, *Lincoln's Rise to the Presidency* (Lawrence: University Press of Kansas, 2006), 197–99; Ecelbarger, *Great Comeback*, 180–82.

9. Harris, *Lincoln's Rise to the Presidency*, 197–99; Ecelbarger, *Great Comeback*, 180–82; "Remarks to Republican State Convention, Decatur, Illinois," in *New York Tribune,* May 22, 1860, in *Collected Works*, 4:48-49; David Herbert Donald, *Lincoln* (New York: Simon and Schuster, 1995), 244–45. Historians disagree on the banner's wording, which referred to a member of the Hanks family and Lincoln's father. I have quoted only that portion on which scholars agree.

10. Donald, *Lincoln*, 246; Lincoln to Trumbull, Springfield, April 7, 1860, in *Collected Works*, 4:40.

11. Michael Burlingame, *Abraham Lincoln: A Life*, 2 vols. (Baltimore: Johns Hopkins University Press, 2008), 1:599–600; Luthin, *First Lincoln Campaign*, 65.

12. Ecelbarger, *Great Comeback*, 187.

13. Lincoln to Mark W. Delahay, Springfield, May 12, 1860, in *Collected Works*, 4:49; Lincoln to Edward Wallace, Springfield, May 12, 1860, in ibid.; "Endorsement on the Margin of the *Missouri Democrat*," [May 17, 1860], in ibid., 4:50.

14. Burlingame, *Abraham Lincoln*, 1:603; Ecelbarger, *Great Comeback*, 192; Reinhard H. Luthin, *The Real Abraham Lincoln: A Complete One-Volume History of His Life and Times* (Englewood Cliffs: Prentice-Hall, 1960), 217.

15. *Chicago Press and Tribune*, May 15, 1860; Willard King, *Lincoln's Manager, David Davis* (Cambridge: Harvard University Press, 1960), 135–36.

16. Glyndon G. Van Deusen, *Thurlow Weed: Wizard of the Lobby* (Boston: Little, Brown, 1947), 250–51; William Butler to Abraham Lincoln, Chicago, May 14, 1860, Lincoln Papers, LC; Ecelbarger, *Great Comeback*, 193.

17. Luthin, *First Lincoln Campaign*, 139.

18. Delahay to Lincoln, Chicago, May 14, 1860, Lincoln Papers, LC; Charles H. Ray to Lincoln, Lincoln Papers, LC; Nathan Knapp to Lincoln, Lincoln Papers, LC; Butler to Lincoln, Chicago, May 14, 1860, Lincoln Papers, LC; Ecelbarger, *Great Comeback*, 193–97; Luthin, *First Lincoln Campaign*, 155. Ray's letter is dated "Monday," which would have been May 14, and makes clear Ray was in Chicago, hence my attribution of date and location.

19. John Wesley North to George Loomis, Chicago, May 15, 1860 box 7, John Wesley North Papers, Henry E. Huntington Library, San Marino, California; Butler to Lincoln, Chicago, May 15, 1860, Lincoln Papers, LC; Davis and Jesse K. Dubois to Lincoln, Lincoln Papers, LC; Dubois to Lincoln, Lincoln Papers, LC; Ecelbarger, *Great Comeback*, 198–99.

20. Ecelbarger, *Great Comeback*, 204–5.

21. William B. Hesseltine, ed., *Three Against Lincoln: Murat Halstead Reports the Caucuses of 1860* (Baton Rouge: Louisiana State University Press, 1960), 144.

22. Ibid.; Van Deusen, *Thurlow Weed*, 251; Delahay to Lincoln, Chicago, May 17, 1860, Lincoln Papers, LC; Judd to Lincoln, Chicago, May 16, 1860, Lincoln Papers, LC; Davis to Lincoln, Chicago, May 17, 1860, Lincoln Papers, LC; Don E. Fehrenbacher, *Lincoln in Text and Context* (Stanford: Stanford University Press, 1987), 56.

23. Ecelbarger, *Great Comeback*, 211.

24. Ray to Lincoln, Chicago, May 14, 1860, Lincoln Papers, LC; Ecelbarger, *Great Comeback*, 196–97, 213–14; Luthin, *First Lincoln Campaign*, 158.

25. David M. Potter, *The Impending Crisis: 1848–1861* (New York: Harper and Row, 1976), 428.

26. Ibid.; Burlingame, *Abraham Lincoln*, 1:611. See Donald, *Lincoln*, 249–50 and the footnotes on 637–38, on the debate over what Davis did or did not do.

27. Burlingame, *Abraham Lincoln*, 1:596–97, 604; Luthin, *First Lincoln Campaign*, 31, 157; Gabor S. Boritt, *Lincoln and the Economics of the American Dream* (Memphis: Memphis State University Press, 1978).

28. Leonard Swett to Lincoln, n.p., May 25, 1860, Lincoln Papers, LC; King, *Lincoln's Manager*, 143–44.

29. Thomas Haines Dudley, "Report on Republican National Convention of 1860; caucuses & C. leading to nomination of Abraham Lincoln," ca. 1875, Thomas Haines Dudley Papers, Henry E. Huntington Library, San Marino, California; John L. Stratton to Dudley, Washington, May 23, 1860, in ibid.

30. Luthin, *First Lincoln Campaign*, 160; Ecelbarger, *Great Comeback*, 221; Douglas L. Wilson and Rodney O. Davis, eds., *Herndon's Informants: Letters, Interviews, and Statements about Abraham Lincoln* (Urbana: University of Illinois Press, 1998), 491; Ronald C. White Jr., *A. Lincoln: A Biography* (New York: Random House, 2009), 326.

31. Hesseltine, *Three Against Lincoln*, 169; Murat Halstead, *Caucuses of 1860: A History of the National Political Conventions of the Current Presidential Campaign . . .* (Columbus: Follett, Foster and Company, 1860), 147; Ecelbarger, *Great Comeback*, 226–27.

32. Burlingame, *Abraham Lincoln*, 1:624; Halstead, *Caucuses of 1860*, 149; Luthin, *First Lincoln Campaign*, 166; Hesseltine, *Three Against Lincoln*, 171.

33. Ecelbarger, *Great Comeback*, 231.

34. Halstead, *Caucuses of 1860*, 151; J. G. Randall, *Lincoln the President: Volume 1—Springfield to Bull Run* (New York: Dodd, Mead and Company, 1945), 169.

35. Ecelbarger, *Great Comeback*, 233–34; *Illinois State Journal*, May 19, 1860, in *Collected Works*, 4:50.

36. Davis to Lincoln, Chicago; Ray, John L. Scripps, and Joseph Medill to Lincoln, Chicago; Knapp to Lincoln, Chicago; Jesse W. Fell to Lincoln, Chicago; Trumbull to Lincoln, Washington; John Wentworth to Lincoln, Chicago, all written May 18, 1860, all in Lincoln Papers, LC.

37. George Ashmun to Lincoln, Chicago, May 18, 1860, ibid.; Carl Schurz, *The Reminiscences of Carl Schurz*, 3 vols. (New York: McClure Publishing, 1907–08), 2:187–88; North to Loomis, Northfield, June 3, 1860, box 7, North Papers; Paul M. Angle, *"Here I Have Lived": A History of Lincoln's Springfield, 1821–1865*, 2nd ed. (Chicago: Abraham Lincoln Book Shop, 1971), 238–40; Joshua Speed to Lincoln, Louisville, May 19, 1860, Lincoln Papers, LC.

38. David Herbert Donald, *"We Are Lincoln Men": Abraham Lincoln and His Friends* (New York: Simon and Schuster, 2003), 29–64; William Lee Miller, *Lincoln's Virtues: An Ethical Biography* (New York: Alfred A. Knopf, 2002), especially 393–403; Douglas L. Wilson, *Lincoln's Sword: The Presidency and the Power of Words* (New York: Random House, 2006), 5.

4. From Candidate to Leader

1. Lincoln to Hannibal Hamlin, Springfield, July 18, 1860, in *The Collected Works of Abraham Lincoln*, ed. Roy P. Basler (hereafter *Collected Works*), 9 vols. (New Brunswick, N.J.: Rutgers University Press, 1953–55), 4:84.
2. Richard Carwardine, *Lincoln* (London: Pearson, 2003), 112.
3. Lincoln to Lyman Trumbull, Springfield, December 11, 1858, in *Collected Works*, 3:344–45.
4. *Congressional Globe*, 36th Cong., 1st sess., January 23, 1860, 553; January 12, 1860, 424–25.
5. Lincoln to Hawkins Taylor, Springfield, April 21, 1860, in *Collected Works*, 4:45; Robert W. Johannsen, *Stephen A. Douglas* (New York: Oxford University Press, 1973), 680–748.
6. William B. Hesseltine, ed., *Three Against Lincoln: Murat Halstead Reports the Caucuses of 1860* (Baton Rouge: Louisiana State University Press, 1960), 25, 54–55.
7. Lincoln to Trumbull, Springfield, May 1, 1860, in *Collected Works*, 4:47; Lincoln to Cyrus W. Allen, Springfield, May 1, 1860, in *Collected Works*, 4:46; Hesseltine, *Three Against Lincoln*, 77–78.
8. *Chicago Press and Tribune*, June 26, 1860; Hesseltine, *Three Against Lincoln*, 263.
9. *Chicago Press and Tribune*, June 25, 1860; *New-York Times*, June 2, 25, and 26, 1860; December 7, 1863.
10. *New-York Times*, June 2, 25, and 26, 1860; December 7, 1863; Lincoln to Simeon Francis, Springfield, August 4, 1860, in *Collected Works*, 4:89–90; Elihu B. Washburne to Lincoln, Washington, June 24, 1860, in Abraham Lincoln Papers, Library of Congress (hereafter Lincoln Papers, LC), Series 1, General Correspondence, 1833–1916, downloaded from http://memory.loc.gov.
11. *Washington National Intelligencer*, February 23, 1860, in Joseph Howard Parks, *John Bell of Tennessee* (Baton Rouge: Louisiana State University Press, 1950), 348–49.
12. Lincoln to Trumbull, Springfield, April 7, 1860, in *Collected Works*, 4:40; Horace Greeley to James S. Pike, New York, February 23, 1860, in James S. Pike, *First Blows of the Civil War* (New York: American News Company, 1879), 499–500.
13. *New York Herald*, May 9, 1860, quoted in Parks, *John Bell*, 353.

14. *New-York Times*, May 7, 1860; Lincoln to Anson G. Henry, Springfield, July 4, 1860, in *Collected Works*, 4:81–82.

15. Carwardine, *Lincoln*, 110; Eric Foner, *Free Soil, Free Labor, Free Men: The Ideology of the Republican Party before the Civil War*, 2nd ed. (New York: Oxford University Press, 1995).

16. Carwardine, *Lincoln*, 110; Willard King, *Lincoln's Manager, David Davis* (Cambridge: Harvard University Press, 1960), 145; Lincoln to Trumbull, Springfield, June 5, 1860, in *Collected Works*, 4:71.

17. Again, Lincoln's original spelling and punctuation are reproduced here (and later in the chapter). Lincoln to Trumbull, Springfield, May 26, 1860, in *Collected Works*, 4:55; King, *Lincoln's Manager*, 144–45; Lincoln to Carl Schurz, Springfield, June 18, 1860, in *Collected Works*, 4:78.

18. Lincoln to James E. Harvey, Springfield, August 14, 1860, in *Collected Works*, 4:94; Lincoln to William H. Seward, n.p., n.d. but ca. July 21, 1860, in *Collected Work*, 4:86; Lincoln to Trumbull, Springfield, June 5, 1860, in *Collected Works*, 4:71; Carwardine, *Lincoln*, 110.

19. Lincoln to Salmon P. Chase, Springfield, May 26, 1860, in *Collected Works*, 4:53.

20. King, *Lincoln's Manager*, 146–47; Reinhard H. Luthin, *The First Lincoln Campaign* (Cambridge: Harvard University Press, 1944), 168.

21. Lincoln to Schuyler Colfax, Springfield, May 26, 1860, in *Collected Works*, 4:54; Lincoln to Colfax, Springfield, May 31, 1860, in ibid., 4:57–58.

22. Lincoln, "Remarks at a Republican Rally, Springfield, Illinois," August 8, 1860, in *Illinois State Journal*, August 9, 1860, in *Collected Works*, 4:91; *Peoria Daily Transcript*, August 13, 1860, in *Collected Works*, 4:91–92, note; Carwardine, *Lincoln*, 111–12; Luthin, *First Lincoln Campaign*, 184.

23. Lincoln to Samuel Haycraft, Springfield, June 4, 1860, in *Collected Works*, 4:69–70; August 16, 1860, in ibid., 4:97; August 23, 1860, in ibid., 4:99; Lincoln to William Cullen Bryant, Springfield, June 28, 1860, in ibid., 4:81; Lincoln to George G. Fogg, Springfield, August 14, 1860, in ibid., 4:94; August 16, 1860, in ibid., 4:96–97; August 29, 1860, in ibid., 4:102; Lincoln to Zachariah Chandler, Springfield, August 31, 1860, in ibid., 4:102–3; Lincoln to J. Mason Haight, Springfield, June 11, 1860, in ibid., 4:75.

24. Lincoln to Joshua Giddings, Springfield, June 26, 1860, in ibid., 4:80–81; Lincoln to Abraham Jonas, Springfield, July 21, 1860, in ibid., 4:85–86; Lincoln to Charles H. Fisher, Springfield, August 27, 1860, in ibid., 4:101; Lincoln to T. Apolion Cheney, Springfield, August 14, 1860, in ibid., 4:93; Lincoln to G. Yoke Tams, Springfield, September 22, 1860, in ibid., 4:119; Lincoln to James H. Reed, Springfield, October 1, 1860, in ibid., 4:124–25.

25. David Donald, *Lincoln's Herndon: A Biography* (New York: Alfred A. Knopf, 1948), 131–43; Lincoln, "Form Reply to Requests for Political Opinions," Springfield, ca. June 1860, in *Collected Works*, 4:60:

26. Carwardine, *Lincoln*, 111–30; Michael F. Holt, *The Rise and Fall of the American Whig Party: Jacksonian Politics and the Onset of Civil War* (New York: Oxford University Press, 1999).

27. Lincoln to Trumbull, Springfield, June 5, 1860, in *Collected Works*, 4:71; King, *Lincoln's Manager*, 150–53.

28. King, *Lincoln's Manager*, 150–53.

29. Lincoln to John M. Pomeroy, Springfield, August 31, 1860, in *Collected Works*, 4:103–4; King, *Lincoln's Manager*, 153–55.

30. King, *Lincoln's Manager*, 147–48.

31. Richard W. Thompson to Lincoln, Terre Haute, June 12 and July 6, 1860, Lincoln Papers, LC; Colfax to Lincoln, Washington, May 26, May 30, June 18, June 25, 1860, Lincoln Papers, LC; King, *Lincoln's Manager*, 148–49; Lincoln to Thompson, Springfield, June 18 and July 10, 1860, in *Collected Works*, 4:79, 82–83.

32. Thompson to Lincoln, Terre Haute, July 6, 1860, Lincoln Papers, LC; Lincoln to Thompson, Springfield, July 10, 1860, in *Collected Works*, 4:82–83; Lincoln to John G. Nicolay, n.p. but Springfield, n.d. but ca. July 16, 1860, in *Collected Works*, 4:83.

33. King, *Lincoln's Manager*, 153.

34. Norman Judd to Lincoln, May 28, 1860, Lincoln Papers, LC; Davis to Lincoln, July 24, 1860, Lincoln Papers, LC; King, *Lincoln's Manager*, 148–53.

35. Lincoln to Leonard Swett, Springfield, May 26, 1860, in *Collected Works*, 4:55.

36. Lincoln to Swett, Springfield, May 30, 1860, in *Collected Works*, 4:57; Lincoln to James O. Putnam, Springfield, July 29 and September 13, 1860, in *Collected Works*, 4:89, 115; King, *Lincoln's Manager*, 147.

37. Lincoln to Trumbull, Springfield, June 5, 1860, in *Collected Works*, 4:71.

38. King, *Lincoln's Manager*, 137. From *Collected Works*: Lincoln to Caleb B. Smith, Springfield, May 26, 1860, 4:55; Lincoln to Harvey, Springfield, June 9, 1860, 4:73; Lincoln to Schurz, Springfield, June 18, 1860, 4:78; Lincoln to Cassius M. Clay, Springfield, July 20, 1860, 4:85; Lincoln to James F. Simmons, Springfield, August 17, 1860, 4:97; Lincoln to Washburne, Springfield, June 17, 1860, 4:77; Lincoln to Hamlin, Springfield, July 18, 1860, 4:84; Lincoln to Simon Cameron, Springfield, August 6, 1860, 4:90–91; Lincoln to John Pettit, Springfield, September 14, 1860, 4:115; Lincoln to Edwin D. Morgan, Springfield, September 20, 1860, 4:116.

39. Lincoln, "Autobiography Written for John L. Scripps," n.p., ca. June 1860, in *Collected Works*, 4:60–67; Lincoln to John L. Scripps, Springfield, June 16, 1860, in *Collected Works*, 77; Lincoln to Samuel Galloway, Springfield, June 19, 1860, in *Collected Works*, 4:79–80; King, *Lincoln's Manager*, 145.

40. Lincoln, "Autobiography Written for John L. Scripps," in *Collected Works*, 4:60–67; King, *Lincoln's Manager*, 145; Carwardine, *Lincoln*, 115.

41. Lincoln to Henry, Springfield, July 4, 1860, in *Collected Works*, 4:81–82.

42. Lincoln to Henry Wilson, Springfield, September 1, 1860, in *Collected Works*, 4:109; Lincoln to Weed, Springfield, August 17, 1860, in *Collected Works*, 4:97–98; Lincoln to Morgan, Springfield, September 20, 1860, in *Collected Works*, 4:116–17; David Herbert Donald, *Lincoln* (New York: Simon and Schuster, 1995), 254.

43. Lincoln to Robert Schenck, Springfield, August 23, 1860, in *Collected Works*, 4:99–100; Lincoln to Hamlin, Springfield, September 4, 1860, in ibid., 4:110; Lincoln to Joseph Medill, Springfield, September 4, 1860, in ibid., 4:110–11; Lincoln to Alexander K. McClure, Springfield, September 6, 1860, in ibid., 4:112–13; Lincoln to Washburne, Springfield, September 9, 1860, in ibid., 4:113–14.

5. The Making of the President, 1860

1. "Fragment on Stephen A. Douglas," ca. December 1856, in *The Collected Works of Abraham Lincoln*, ed. Roy P. Basler (hereafter *Collected Works*), 9 vols. (New Brunswick, N.J.: Rutgers University Press, 1953–55), 2:382–83; Paul Simon, *Lincoln's Preparation for Greatness: The Illinois Legislative Years* (Norman: University of Oklahoma Press, 1965), 110; Roy Morris Jr., *The Long Pursuit: Abraham Lincoln's Thirty-Year Struggle with Stephen Douglas for the Heart and Soul of America* (New York: HarperCollins, 2008).

2. Robert W. Johannsen, *Stephen A. Douglas* (New York: Oxford University Press, 1973), 783; Sean Wilentz, *The Rise of American Democracy: Jefferson to Lincoln* (New York: W. W. Norton, 2005), 763–64; William C. Harris, *Lincoln's Rise to the Presidency* (Lawrence: University Press of Kansas, 2006), 227–28.

3. Johannsen, *Stephen A. Douglas*, 797–800; Allan Nevins, *The Emergence of Lincoln*, vol. 2, *Prologue to Civil War* (New York: Charles Scribner's Sons, 1950), 295.

4. Michael F. Holt, *The Rise and Fall of the American Whig Party: Jacksonian Politics and the Onset of Civil War* (New York: Oxford University Press, 1999), 39–40.

5. Hiram Barney to Norman B. Judd, New York, September 24, 1860, box 2, folder 42, Barney Papers, Henry E. Huntington Library, San Marino, California. See also David M. Potter, *The Impending Crisis: 1848–1861* (New York: Harper and Row, 1976), 438; and William Lee Miller, *Lincoln's Virtues: An Ethical Biography* (New York: Alfred A. Knopf, 2002), 465–67.

6. Glyndon G. Van Deusen, *Horace Greeley: Nineteenth Century Crusader* (Philadelphia: University of Pennsylvania Press, 1953), 252; Henry D. Bacon to S. L. M. Barlow, St. Louis, October 9, 1860, box 32, A-B, Barlow Papers, Henry E. Huntington Library, San Marino, California; John Slidell to Barlow, New Orleans, October 17, 1860, box 35, 1860, P-S, Barlow Papers; Senate Chamber, June 27, 1860, in Barlow Papers; Austin Baldwin to John A. Rockwell, New York, July 5, 1860, box 36, May-September 1860, Rockwell Collection, Henry E. Huntington Library, San Marino, California; T. J. Barnett to Rockwell, Buffalo, July 9, 1860, Rockwell Collection; Benjamin Ogle Taylor to John Rockwell, Tracy, September 26, 1860, Rockwell Collection; Johannsen, *Stephen A. Douglas*, 787–88; Joseph Howard Parks, *John Bell of Tennessee* (Baton Rouge: Louisiana State University Press, 1950), 363–64.

7. Parks, *John Bell*, 376–88.

8. Lincoln to Thurlow Weed, Springfield, August 17, 1860, in *Collected Works*, 4:97–98; Emerson D. Fite, *The Presidential Campaign of 1860* (New York: Macmillan, 1911), 223.

9. Barney to Judd, New York, September 24, 1860, box 2, folder 42, Barney Papers. S. H. White to Rockwell, Hartford, January 29, 1860, box 35, August 1859–April 1860 (although dated January, it appears to have been written in June); Charles R. Alsop to Rockwell, Middletown, August 25, 1860, box 36, May–September 1860; Osmyn Baker to Rockwell, Northampton, September 26, 1860, box 36; J. R. Ingersoll to Rockwell, Philadelphia, October 5, 1860, box 37, May–September 1860; Benjamin Ogle Taylor to John Rockwell, Tracy, September 26, 1860, box 36, all in Rockwell Collection. James T. Brady to Barlow, New York, September 24, 1860, box 31, 1860, A-B, Barlow Papers; Wilentz, *Rise of American Democracy*, 764.

10. John Dunham to Rockwell, Norwich, August 30, 1860, box 36, Rockwell Papers; John W. Allen to Rockwell, Cleveland, September 26, 1860, box 36, Rockwell Papers; John Breckinridge to Barlow, Washington, June 30, 1860, box 31, 1860, A-B, Barlow Papers; William M. Browne to Barlow, Washington, July 1, 1860, box 31, 1860, A-B, Barlow Papers; Johannsen, *Stephen A. Douglas*, 787–88.

11. Wilentz, *Rise of American Democracy*, 763; Johannsen, *Stephen A. Douglas*, 778, 792–93.

12. *New-York Daily Times*, August 4 and 16, 1860; *New York Weekly Tribune*, September 8, 1860; Johannsen, *Stephen A. Douglas*, 783–84; Nevins, *Emergence of Lincoln*, 2:285.

13. Wilentz, *Rise of American Democracy*, 762; Roy F. Nichols, *The Disruption of American Democracy* (New York: Free Press, 1948), 332–37; Jesse Bright to Barlow, Washington, June 30 and July 19, 1860, box 31, 1860, A-B, Barlow Papers.

14. Johannsen, *Stephen A. Douglas*, 779, 795; Nevins, *Emergence of Lincoln*, 2:293; Nichols, *Disruption of American Democracy*, 343.

15. Michael Burlingame, *Abraham Lincoln: A Life*, 2 vols. (Baltimore: Johns Hopkins University Press, 2008), 1:629–30.

16. Lincoln to Anson G. Henry, Springfield, September 22, 1860, in *Collected Works*, 4:118; Lincoln to Francis E. Spinner, Springfield, September 24, 1860, in *Collected Works*, 4:120; James E. Harvey to Lincoln, September 22, 1860, Series 1, General Correspondence, 1833–1916, Abraham Lincoln Papers, Library of Congress (hereafter Lincoln Papers, LC), downloaded from http://memory.loc.gov; Lincoln to Harvey, Springfield, September 27, 1860, in *Collected Works*, 4:122.

17. David Herbert Donald, *Lincoln* (New York: Simon and Schuster, 1995), 337; Lincoln to Edwin D. Morgan, Springfield, September 20, 1860, in *Collected Works*, 4:116; Lincoln to Benjamin F. James, Springfield, September 26, 1860, in *Collected Works*, 4:121.

18. *Chicago Press and Tribune*, October 2 and 3, 1860; Doris Kearns Goodwin, *Team of Rivals: The Political Genius of Abraham Lincoln* (New York: Simon and Schuster, 2005), 270; Lincoln to William H. Seward, Springfield, October 12, 1860, in *Collected Works*, 4:126–27; Davis to Lincoln, Clinton, October 5, 1860, Lincoln Papers, LC; Burlingame, *Abraham Lincoln*, 1:653–56; Reinhard H. Luthin, *The First Lincoln Campaign* (Cambridge: Harvard University Press, 1944), 185.

19. Lincoln to Joseph Medill, Springfield, September 4, 1860, in *Collected Works*, 4:110–11; Judd to Barney, Chicago, September 11, 1860, box 19, folder 26, Barney Papers; Barney to Judd, New York, September 17, 1860, box 2, folder 42, Barney Papers.

20. Willard King, *Lincoln's Manager, David Davis* (Cambridge: Harvard University Press, 1960), 158; Nichols, *Disruption of American Democracy*, 359; James A. Bayard to Barlow, Wilmington, October 4, 1860, box 31, 1860, A-B, Barlow Papers.

21. Burlingame, *Abraham Lincoln*, 1:671; Lincoln to Seward, Springfield, October 12, 1860, in *Collected Works*, 4:126–27; Lincoln to John M. Read, Springfield, October 13, 1860, in *Collected Works*, 4:127; Goodwin, *Team of Rivals*, 273–74.

22. Lincoln to William H. Herndon, Springfield, October 10, 1860, in *Collected Works*, 4:126, note; *Chicago Press and Tribune*, October 13, 1860.

23. Ward Hill Lamon to Lincoln, Clinton, October 10, 1860, in Lincoln Papers, LC; Lamon, Note, August 3, 1860, Lamon Papers, box 1, Henry E. Huntington Library, San Marino, California.

24. *Chicago Press and Tribune*, October 13, 1860; Alexander McClure to Lincoln, Chambersberg, October 19, 1860, Lincoln Papers, LC; Mark W. Delahay to Lincoln, Lawrenceburg, Indiana, October 10, 1860, Lincoln Papers, LC; Caleb Smith to Lincoln, Indianapolis, October 10, 1860, Lincoln Papers, LC; Carl Schurz to Lincoln, Watertown, October 10, 1860, Lincoln Papers, LC.

25. King, *Lincoln's Manager*, 159; Simeon Draper, Republican State Committee Circular, Albany, October 18, 1860, Lincoln Papers, LC.

26. Elihu Washburne to Lincoln, Galena, October 22, 1860, Lincoln Papers, LC.

27. Lincoln to George T. M. Davis, Springfield, October 27, 1860, in *Collected Works*, 4:132–33; Lincoln to George G. Fogg, Springfield, October 31, 1860, in *Collected Works*, 4:135–36; Lincoln to David Hunter, Springfield, October 26, 1860, in *Collected Works*, 4:132; Lincoln to L. Montgomery Bond, Springfield, October 15, 1860, in *Collected Works*, 4:128; Lincoln to William S. Speer, Springfield, October 23, 1860, in *Collected Works*, 4:130; Lincoln to George D. Prentice and Lincoln to David Hunter, Springfield, October 29, 1860, in *Collected Works*, 4:134–35; Hunter to Lincoln, Fort Leavenworth, November 1, 1860, Lincoln Papers, LC.

28. Nichols, *Disruption of American Democracy*, 359; Nevins, *Emergence of Lincoln*, 2:311.

29. Johannsen, *Stephen A. Douglas*, 788–800; Nevins, *Emergence of Lincoln*, 2:295; Wilentz, *Rise of American Democracy*, 763.

30. *Chicago Press and Tribune*, October 2, 1860; Davis to Lincoln, Urbana, October 31, 1860, Lincoln Papers, LC; Johannsen, *Stephen A. Douglas*, 785; Reinhard H. Luthin, *The Real Abraham Lincoln: A Complete One-Volume History of His Life and Times* (Englewood Cliffs: Prentice-Hall, 1960), 235.

31. Richard Carwardine, "Lincoln's Religion," in *Our Lincoln: New Perspectives on Lincoln and His World*, ed. Eric Foner (New York: W. W. Norton, 2008), 236; Daniel Walker Howe, *The Political Culture of the American Whigs* (Chicago: University of Chicago Press, 1979); Mark Noll, "American Religion, 1809–1865," in *Lincoln's America, 1809–1865*, ed. Joseph R. Fornieri and Sara Vaughn Gabbard (Carbondale: Southern Illinois University Press, 2008), 72–93.

32. Burlingame, *Abraham Lincoln*, 1:676–77; David Donald, *Lincoln's Herndon: A Biography* (New York: Alfred A. Knopf, 1948), 143; Luthin, *Real Abraham Lincoln*, 237; Donald, *Lincoln*, 255.

33. Gregory A. Borchard, "From Pink Lemonade to Salt River: Horace Greeley's Utopia and the Death of the Whig Party," *Journalism History* 32:1 (Spring 2006): 22–33, explains the metaphor; Burlingame, *Abraham Lincoln*, 1:677–78.

34. Harold Holzer, *Lincoln President-Elect: Abraham Lincoln and the Great Secession Winter, 1860–1861* (New York: Simon and Schuster, 2008), 35–38 and 503, note 135; Goodwin, *Team of Rivals*, 276–77; Morris, *Long Pursuit*, 194; Donald, *Lincoln*, 255–56; Nevins, *Emergence of Lincoln*, 2:314–15; Luthin, *Real Abraham Lincoln*, 237; Burlingame, *Abraham Lincoln*, 1:678–79.

35. Jean H. Baker, *Mary Todd Lincoln: A Biography* (New York: W. W. Norton, 1987), 161–62; Ronald C. White Jr., *A. Lincoln: A Biography* (New York: Random House, 2009), 347; Paul M. Angle, *"Here I Have Lived": A History of Lincoln's Springfield, 1821–1865*, 2nd ed. (Chicago: Abraham Lincoln Book Shop, 1971), 251–53; Kenneth J. Winkle, "The Middle-Class Marriage of Abraham and Mary Lincoln," in *Lincoln's America*, 94; Holzer, *Lincoln President-Elect*, 44–45.

36. Judd to Barney, Chicago, November 11, 1860, box 19, folder 26, Barney Papers; Holzer, *Lincoln President-Elect*, 45, 58–60; Donald, *Lincoln*, 255–56; Stephen B. Oates, *With Malice toward None: The Life of Abraham Lincoln* (New York: Harper and Row, 1978), 195; Fogg to Lincoln, New York, November 7, 1860, Lincoln Papers, LC; Salmon P. Chase to Lincoln, Columbus, November 7, 1860, Lincoln Papers, LC.

37. Lincoln to Hamlin, Springfield, November 8, 1860, in *Collected Works*, 4:136; Lincoln to Winfield Scott, Springfield, November 9, 1860, in ibid., 4:137; Lincoln to Truman Smith, Springfield, November 10, 1860, in ibid., 4:138.

38. John Bigelow to William Hargreaves, New York, November 10, 1860, in Burlingame, *Abraham Lincoln*, 1:680.

39. Harris, *Lincoln's Rise to the Presidency*, 243.

40. Wilentz, *Rise of American Democracy*, 765; Johannsen, *Stephen A. Douglas*, 803–4; Potter, *Impending Crisis*, 442; Don E. Fehrenbacher, *Prelude to Greatness: Lincoln in the 1850s* (Stanford: Stanford University Press, 1962), 160.

41. Luthin, *First Lincoln Campaign*, 193–94; James E. Hendrickson, *Joe Lane of Oregon: Machine Politics and the Sectional Crisis, 1849–1861* (New Haven: Yale University Press, 1967), 235–37; Leonard L. Richards, *The California Gold Rush and the Coming of the Civil War* (New York: Random House, 2007).

42. Glyndon G. Van Deusen, *Thurlow Weed: Wizard of the Lobby* (Boston: Little, Brown, and Company, 1947), 258; White, *A. Lincoln*, 343; Harris, *Lincoln's Rise to the Presidency*, 225; Jon Grinspan, "'Young Men for War': The Wide Awakes and Lincoln's 1860 Presidential Campaign," *Journal of American History* 96.2 (September 2009): 357–78; William E. Gienapp, "Who Voted for Lincoln?" in *Abraham Lincoln and the American Political Tradition*, ed. John L. Thomas (Amherst: University of Massachusetts Press, 1986), 58.

43. *Chicago Press and Tribune*, September 5, 1860; Grinspan, "'Young Men for War,'" 365–66; *New York Daily Tribune*, May 11, 1860, in Peter Knupfer, "Aging Statesmen and the Statesmanship of an Earlier Age: The Generational Roots of the Constitutional Union Party," in *Union and Emancipation: Essays on Politics and Race in the Civil War Era*, ed. David W. Blight and Brooks D. Simpson (Kent: Kent State University Press, 1997), 59; Gienapp, "Who Voted For Lincoln?" 61.

44. Van Deusen, *Horace Greeley*, 249, 252–53; Potter, *Impending Crisis*, 418.

45. Jeter Allen Isely, *Horace Greeley and the Republican Party, 1853–1861: A Study of the New York Tribune* (Princeton: Princeton University Press, 1947), 266.

46. William W. Freehling, *The Road to Disunion*, vol. 2, *Secessionists Triumphant, 1854–1861* (New York: Oxford University Press, 2007), 330; Morris, *Long Pursuit*, 187; Potter, *Impending Crisis*, 432, 442–43; Burlingame, *Abraham Lincoln*, 1:675.

47. Burlingame, *Abraham Lincoln*, 1:635–38.

48. Gienapp, "Who Voted For Lincoln?" 63; Luthin, *First Lincoln Campaign*, 184; Nichols, *Disruption of American Democracy*, 367; Harris, *Lincoln's Rise to the Presidency*, 227; Eric Foner, *Free Soil, Free Labor, Free Men: The Ideology of the Republican Party before the Civil War*, 2nd ed. (New York: Oxford University Press, 1995), 216–18; Parks, *John Bell*, 363.

49. Holzer, *Lincoln President-Elect*, 45.

INDEX

Michael S. Green is professor of history at the College of Southern Nevada, where he teaches U.S. and Nevada history. He is the author of *Freedom, Union, and Power: Lincoln and His Party during the Civil War*; *Politics and America in Crisis: The Coming of the Civil War*; and numerous other books and articles.

CONCISE
LINCOLN
LIBRARY

This series of concise books fills a need for short studies of the life, times, and legacy of President Abraham Lincoln. Each book gives readers the opportunity to quickly achieve basic knowledge of a Lincoln-related topic. These books bring fresh perspectives to well-known topics, investigate previously overlooked subjects, and explore in greater depth topics that have not yet received book-length treatment. For a complete list of current and forthcoming titles, see www.conciselincolnlibrary.com.

Other Books in the Concise Lincoln Library

Abraham Lincoln and Horace Greeley
Gregory A. Borchard

Lincoln and the Civil War
Michael Burlingame

Abraham and Mary Lincoln
Kenneth J. Winkle